What Others Are Saying About *WHEN FAITH DARES*

"*When Faith Dares* is a bold, rich, rewarding, and revealing read. You will be blessed and challenged! Terri McFarland unabashedly invites us into her journey of faith, the highs and lows and all in between. Through it all she identifies the finger of God at work on so many levels and so many ways. In boldly sharing her life journey of *daring* faith, you not only hear the story of a maturing magnificent Christian, but you meet Jesus as the "Word becomes flesh" in and through Terri's life."

—George DeJong
Author of *In A Word*
Founder of Under The Fig Tree Ministries

"Many a believer struggles with their faith in many a valley. We get discouraged, we grow weary and often times never reach those mountaintops His heart desires for those He loves. With honesty and candor, Terri takes you to those places in *When Faith Dares*. You can't help but want to go higher and holier when you read the stories, scriptures and life lessons in this book."

—Kathy Troccoli
Singer, Songwriter, Author

"*When Faith Dares* can be defined in one word: transformational. Terri didn't merely write this story, she lived it first. The depth of transformation Terri has traversed in her journey spurs deep change in my life – and it will in yours too."

—Scott Staal
Coaches Ministry Strategist
for the Fellowship of Christian Athletes

"We all face times where life is hard and we want to check out in some way. What we need to realize is these moments are an invitation we don't want to miss for our faith to be strengthened. On the pages of this book, Terri leads us to respond to that invitation and find the kind of steadying faith that anchors us even when the winds of life blow."

—Jill Savage
Host of the No More Perfect Podcast
and author of *Real Moms...Real Jesus*

WHEN FAITH DARES

Discover the Power of Courage to Stay the Course
When You'd Rather Bail

Terri McFarland

EABooks Publishing
Your Partner In Publishing

Cover design by: Heidi Harrington
Author photos by: Pat & Cassie Photography, Crown Point, IN

ISBN: 978-1-955309-30-1
LCCN: 2023901148

Published by EA Books Publishing, a division of
Living Parables of Central Florida, Inc. a 501c3
EABooksPublishing.com

*My life continues to be profoundly influenced by the daring
faith of my parents, Armour and Siola McFarland, who showed me
how to hold on to Jesus amid inevitable disappointment.
I am richly blessed—and joyfully anticipate the day
we will all sing together again.*

TABLE OF CONTENTS

Chapter 1

DARING TO DREAM

The brisk morning breeze tousled my hair as I climbed the creaky planks to our backyard tree house. Swaying branches from the oak tree filtered the sun's rays into shapes that pranced like circus animals across the wood siding. Ten feet up I escaped the clamor and ruckus of my three siblings. Far from unwelcomed distractions, my vivid imagination ran wild. For what seemed like hours, I pictured myself soaring above the clouds, living in a castle, and running so fast my brothers would never catch me. Up here, I felt invisible to the world. I believed anything was possible and climbed that tree every chance I could. Gazing at the clouds in wonderment, I was oblivious to the divine dreams growing within me as faith poured into my soul.

Then one day, my parents moved our family to another city, and I struggled to replicate the space where my imaginings ruled and *daring* dreams flourished. The simplicity of childhood soon became a distant memory as my adolescent attention turned to school, sports, music, relationships, and a career choice. It no longer felt right to fill my afternoons picturing stuffed animals coming to life, a prince rescuing my dolls, or basketball shots that won championships.

The hours spent studying, practicing sports, singing, dating, and prepping for work, however, began to feel rote, as though I were merely going through the motions. Professors, coaches, and employers fervently redirected my focus, and my innocent wonder gradually disappeared. Gone were my precious days to dream. I soon became engrossed in the rapid completion of activities, as though I was simply ticking items off a list. Even my faith became a rut of routine: go to church, read my Bible (the Text), spend time in prayer . . . *repeat.*

The God-inspired dreams of my youth kept me from being satisfied with mediocrity. As a result, my methodical (and too often predictable) lifestyle battled a yearning for an experience that echoed the Bible stories of Joseph, who through persecution and perceived failure held on to a divine dream, and Esther, who willingly put her life on the line to risk following God's plan.

How daring! I thought. *I want that kind of courage to be characteristic of me.*

I pored over the biographies of faith-filled men and women, like Corrie ten Boom, Brother Andrew, Dietrich Bonhoeffer, Nicky Cruz, and Joni Erickson Tada. Who *dared* to hide Jews, smuggle Bibles, fight for freedom, pursue love, and conquer physical limitations. They set out to transform their world. And reminiscent of the thrill that pulsed through my own early dreams of love, triumph, and superhero-like abilities, their lives were anything but conventional. I was hooked. Secretly I prayed my life would reflect similar *daring* choices. That one day I would willingly follow an uncommon path involving a distinct element of risk. But in that moment, I was just an ordinary person going about my ordinary days, living an ordinary life. What would *daring* faith look like for me?

The daughter of a pastor, I had grown up feeling secure and comfortable (if you call spending a *lot* of time in church comfortable—let's just say it was my normal). Our family read the Text at the dinner table, sang in four-part harmony around the piano, and knelt together in prayer before bed. While I knew faith was necessary to trust in an invisible God, *daring* in faith was something altogether different. And I wanted something more. Something more fearless. More authentic. More vibrant. I wanted my life to be provocative.

Faith that *dares* involves the willingness to be audaciously bold, courageous, vulnerable, and devoted, all while threatened by the distinct possibility of failure. It calls for us to say "I'm all in" to God, even when we would much rather bail. When we'd much rather do what's easy and what feels good rather than what we know would be life-giving. *Daring* faith requires us to trust—at times blindly—that nothing happens in our world outside of God's influence or authority.

The possibility of an exhilarating quest took hold of me. I believed in the goodness of God and that He had good in mind for me. I sang songs in church to proclaim my devotion, that "though none go with me, still I will follow." But *daring* faith goes deeper. It seizes all those things we say, believe, or sing about and puts them to the test. God was readying me to leave comfortable to step into *daring*.

Before long, I discovered that those childhood dreams of adventure and *daring* pursuits prepared me for the unexpected and devastating losses and circumstances that came my way. And I needed faith—but not just ordinary faith; bold faith. I didn't understand all of God's plan, and without having all the details, I wanted to bail. I figured I could do life just as well on my own.

But like those I read about, the Lord was calling me to embody a faith that *dares*. A *daring* faith that doesn't ask God to anoint my agenda but instead *dares* to follow His. Would I *dare* trust Him to lead when I didn't know the destination? Would I *dare* believe He is good amid the crushing disappointment of broken dreams? The Lord created me with a plan in mind—and that plan was about to require me to risk my comfort, my security, and my reputation to trust Him.

Along this journey, I discovered that *daring* to dream and believe that God is who He says He is and that He will do what He says He will do, the Lord drew me into a deeper relationship with Him. He infused me with undeniable hope right when I did face despair and I was ready to bail on everything and give up. He reignited my heart, which unknowingly ached for His love, His connection, and His purpose. And as I grew closer to the Lord, the more I found He too, is *daringly* unpredictable.

Have you been there? Tired of the ordinary of life and wanting something different, something special—a true adventure? Or perhaps you've faced devastation and felt ready to bail on everything because nothing seems to be going well—even your faith? You'd much rather default to anything that takes away the pain. Maybe you desire to reconnect with the Lord yet it's a daunting proposition to *dare* look beyond your current circumstance. To *dare* let go of what you rely on to trust God's plan.

What I learned—and what I believe is true for you too—is that God wants us to overcome, to dig in our heels and to trust Him with everything we've got. In short, He wants us to courageously *dare* to follow Him—in the good times, of course (but that's the easy stuff, right?), but more importantly when everything within us wants to bail—when we feel the most blindsided, lost, or hopeless. That's *daring* faith. That's letting God chart our course for the unknown, trusting that He is in it *all*—and will work it all out ultimately for our good— even when we can't see or understand where He is leading.

The Ultimate Goal of Having *Daring* Faith

At its core, *daring* faith depicts a love story. And the more we practice boldly trusting God, the more we will experience His loving grace and tender mercy. As Jesus anchors our hope and emboldens our spirit, our desire to know Him intimately will take root and flourish. For the fulfillment of a vision or of a dream is not the final pursuit. Falling in love with Jesus as we *dare* chase after His heart is the ultimate goal.

God wants us to embrace the faith to *dare* greatly and imagine wildly, as though peering through the rickety boards of a backyard tree fort. And with wonder-filled, childlike faith, we will learn to hold on to Jesus in that sacred place where we really don't understand what's happening, where He is leading us, or why it's taking so long to get what we're longing for.

Perhaps your childhood innocence disappeared long ago and the ensuing path is strewn with broken trust and shattered relationships. Perhaps you were forced to grow up quickly, and now, a well-intentioned grownup, you find yourself caught in situations that make *daring* to step out in faith to dream both arduous and painful. How do you walk in faith when your heart has been trampled and you struggle to hope? How do you renew your confidence in the Lord's power, grace, and unexpected strength when life doesn't turn out as you expect?

When Faith Dares is my story of heartbreak, loss, and the cultivation of *daring* courage. If you wrestle with God in the valley and wonder how you will make it through, then you will resonate with my experience. Hope will come. And together we can be encouraged to follow Jesus even as dreams are reduced to rubble and bailing seems like the better option. Together we can be emboldened to *break through* roadblocks, *step out* in faith, and *stay the course*—even when it defies logic. For absent of risk, a *dare* is meaningless.

Jesus offered an imaginative, audacious invitation to a handful of eager young men: "Follow me, and I will make you fishers of men."[1] Not knowing where it would lead, they *dared* to believe and chose to track with Jesus.

The same choice exists for you and me today.

Now decades beyond sunny afternoons high in a tree fort, what had become rote and absent of feeling has forged back to life as a *daring* faith in God refines my life by the day. Through the power of His presence and His love, I came to know it is entirely possible to authentically live out what I say I believe, even when navigating an intense and lonely wilderness filled with life-altering obstacles.

Let us discover how to trust the Lord with expectant and imaginative faith. To *dare* envision what we can't see, to *dare* to believe in a loving God, and to *dare* to obey His Word. Let us *dare* to listen for His voice, *dare* to hope in the middle of disappointment, and *dare* to endure when we feel ill-equipped and know that the road is long. And even if what we *dare* dream or pray for never comes true in this lifetime, God's plan will prevail. Amid the unexpected detours, His presence and His Word will instill within us the power of courage and transform us into something absolutely beautiful.

Chapter 2

It's Going to Look Impossible

A lunchtime drive across town provided a welcomed break from the demands of the classroom. As a high school teacher readily feeding off the energy of teenagers, my days were full and ever changing. The gift of a few quiet moments let me unwind and begin to process my latest heartache. Two days earlier, my boyfriend told me he no longer thought it was going to work out between us. I was still reeling. I assumed we were heading toward engagement. The resulting break up left me feeling discarded and questioning whether my husband would ever find me. I wondered if God really cared about this part of my life.

I grabbed a sandwich and drove to a nearby lake. Watching the waves rise and fall on passing boats mirrored the ebb and flow of my own loneliness.

"Where is my life heading, Lord? I really don't understand the plan," I blurted out loud.

Now in my thirties, frustration hit a fever pitch as I watched friends walk down the aisle and start families when I couldn't keep a relationship going. While grateful for the opportunity to teach, coach, and occasionally delve into the music industry, my unrequited quest for marriage (and subsequent relationship failures) took its toll. I wearied of trying to encounter godly, eligible men and wondered how I kept messing up something so simple. In that moment of brokenness, the Lord impressed upon my spirit words that would change me forever.

Relax, He said. You're to marry Mitch Carver. And it's going to look impossible.

Mitch Carver? I thought. What does he have to do with anything? I'm trying to process why my last beau stepped away, not think about some random guy I barely know.

"Lord, was that really You I just heard?" I whispered out loud. "And did You just say I am to marry Mitch Carver?" At that moment, I heard nothing else. But a sudden peace poured over my spirit eradicating the sting of rejection. This was not the first time the Lord downloaded words to my heart, so the notion that He spoke wasn't as shocking as what I heard. However, His response to my exasperation answered a question I didn't ask. Mitch and I had crossed paths at a community event a few years ago, but we hardly knew each other. Why would I marry him? I thought confirmation from the Lord about whom to marry came after a prolonged and committed relationship. The pain of my recent breakup slowly took a back seat as I became fixated on what I just heard. My stomach swirled at the potential implications.

Relax? Right. Is this a joke?

The warm sun and the gentle wind off the lake, while refreshing, failed to calm my spirit as my mind started to battle my heart. I immediately considered dismissing what I heard as some sort of irrational musing—except those words would have never crossed my mind. Ever.

Lord, help me here!

Although it had been years since the stoking of my imagination high up in a tree, I was compelled to consider the Spirit might be placing a vision in my soul *daring* me to trust His prompting. I often prayed for my routine schedule of classes and practices to one day be interrupted by a God moment of sorts. Maybe this was it. My eyes filled with tears. What began as a longing for a simple word of encouragement to stop my descent into a pit of despair, turned into something totally unexpected. God's words resonated deep within my soul. I lingered by the water a little longer to pull myself together before going back to work.

I wanted to somehow corroborate what happened but that was impossible. I was alone. And as an educator in a public school, sharing my lunch-hour experience with coworkers would garner intense skepticism. There was no way to adequately express, "Do you know that while I sat out by the lake God told me whom He wants me to marry?" without colleagues discounting everything I said for the next ten years. They would think I was nuts. I wondered that myself. In a daze I drove back to school with the words God conveyed stuck on replay.

Relax. You're to marry Mitch Carver. And it's going to look impossible.

The first part of what I heard hijacked my thoughts because the second half I understood. Marrying Mitch already looked impossible, felt crazy, and made no sense. And since my perception of how other people viewed me often steered my decision-making process, I hesitated to tell my family or close friends what had occurred.

Days passed and I found myself unable to ignore what the Lord had poured into my heart—and I really tried. I felt as if I was attempting to stop a cascading river by standing in the middle of it. Voices of doubt relentlessly spun in my head. *Did I hear right? Did I hear at all? How can I be sure this word to my spirit came from the Lord? None of my friends have shared anything similar. If it truly is the Lord, why tell me now and like this? Couldn't He have spoken to my heart after Mitch and I were at least talking? Seems more reasonable to me.*

Repeated rationalizations made it hard to concentrate on much else. Maybe it was a dream, wishful thinking, or a really bad sandwich. Or maybe the enemy was posing again. He is such a master of deceit.

But something (better said, Someone) *dared* me to believe that the words echoing in my mind, pounding through my heart, and consuming my prayers were true. Even though I wouldn't think twice about hiking through the woods alone or blindly jumping off a high dive, the reality of this unnerving experience required a much broader imagination than I currently possessed. I craved reassurance.

Lord, did I hear You right? Would You mind repeating Yourself just so I can be sure?

Nothing.

Of course, the silence only fueled my doubt. The words continued to revolve as I tried to find something I missed. Did God say I was *going* to marry Mitch, or that I *might* marry Mitch? Maybe He asked what I *thought* about marrying Mitch? Or that He would *like* it if I married Mitch?

Did I hear the name right? Was it Mitch? Or was it Matthew? Or Martin, or Marcus, or Maximillian? (Okay, I'm pretty sure it wasn't that one.) Everything started to blur. I eagerly anticipated the joy of a Christ-honoring marriage, but I never pictured it starting out like this.

It wasn't as if I opposed the idea of Mitch. His confidence and love for Jesus was curiously captivating. However, our circle of friends seldom overlapped, which made our brief conversations typical of acquaintances. I never considered him anything more and leaned toward writing off this recent occurrence as a fabrication of my mind. Just forget I went out for lunch, forget about Mitch, forget trying to listen for God's tender voice. That might be the better play. After all, no one knew about it but me.

Or I could just wait and see if this panned out rather than risk my reputation by sharing what would take a vivid imagination to even process. Besides, I was sure the conservative church I'd grown up in and my current community would quickly dismiss this entire incident out-of-hand. They believed the only way God speaks to us today is through the Bible—don't subtract from it and certainly don't add to it. (I was a bit of an aberration.) That left me with a conundrum. Either I live as though the Lord said those words, or I safely ignore the risk of a potentially uncontrollable outcome and go on my way.

Sometimes embracing a faith that *dares* requires a willingness to imagine God could lead us to places that at first glance appear impossible. But it's easy to lose our ability to imagine and doubt God is pursuing us or that He is even taking notice. And we get stuck. Our hearts disengage because we won't *dare* to believe in what is not yet real or that our ideas are anything more than just that. Ours. Many of us experience moments in which we are impressed to reach out to a friend, to be more generous, or to refrain from sharing our opinions, and we question whether those thoughts really came from the Lord. We might sense a gentle prodding from the Holy Spirit, to pray for those who have hurt us or to choose to follow Jesus even when it's hard, and we push it aside. We couldn't picture restoration. We couldn't envision the outcome.

The ability to recognize His still small voice and believe His Word is true requires tapping into our God-given imagination: to form a picture in our mind of something not perceived by any of our five senses.

The Power of Divine Imagination

As a child, I remember watching the movie *Willy Wonka & the Chocolate Factory* where Willy, played by Gene Wilder, brought to life a breathtaking world of candy—from supersized red licorice rolls to an array of multicolored lollipops larger than a person's head. In a single wonder-filled moment, Willy opens a door into a world where a handful of wide-eyed children see their imagination come to life. It is a child's dream. As I watched the story unfold, I wished such a place existed. Even now, the enchantment of it all delights me.

Oh, the joy of childhood imaginings.

Screenwriters and novelists inspire us to imagine the improbable. But they aren't the only ones who create worlds of *daring* possibilities. God did it first and He continues to instill within us all the ability to create and imagine something remarkable. He initially displayed to us the vastness of His own imagination in Genesis 1:3 when "God said, 'Let there be light,' and there was light." He saw light before it came to be and when it was done, He thought it was good. Nine times in the very first chapter of Genesis we find the words *And God said*, followed by a fulfillment of what He imagined. He even created us in His own *image*. It doesn't get more *image*-inative than that!

Consider what else we find in the first book of the Bible. Abram (Abraham) needed a vast imagination to embrace a *daring* faith. In Genesis 15:5-6, it says that God "brought [Abram] outside and said, 'Look toward heaven, and number the stars, if you are able to number them.' Then he said to him, 'So shall your offspring be.' And he believed the Lord, and he counted it to him as righteousness." The Lord gave Abram an extraordinary opportunity to *dare* imagine what He said would come to pass.

What sounds like a clear word from the Lord to Abram may not have seemed that way to him at the time (although a physical manifestation of God might be pretty convincing). Abram was getting on in years as was Sarai (Sarah), his wife. They tried for decades to have children to no avail. In a Bedouin culture where children reflect the favor of the Lord, Sarai felt the shame. Having a child hardly appeared viable, but Abram ignored the obvious and chose to believe a radical word. The Lord encouraged him to use his God-given imagination to *dare* believe his offspring would outnumber the stars in the sky and to picture what was not yet real to any of his senses. Although both the Lord and Abram knew that in his lifetime, he would never see the fulfillment of what he was being promised and asked to imagine, Abram *dared* in faith to walk it out anyway.

Will we *dare* to do the same? As the Lord did with Abram, He gives us permission to imagine the possibilities and then provides a way for us to walk in it. In Isaiah 43:19, the Lord says, "Behold, I am doing a new thing; now it springs forth, do you not perceive it? I will make a way in the wilderness and rivers in the desert." God created us with imagination, and He *dares* us to use it. He *dares* us to believe the word He is placing in our hearts. Because divine imagination, the gift God abundantly bestows on His image bearers, has creative power and strength.

You may remember the story in the Bible of a group of people living in the land of Shinar who were trying to make a name for themselves by building a tower to reach the heavens: "The Lord said, Behold, the people is one, and they have all one language; and this they begin to do: and now nothing will be restrained from them, which they have *imagined* to do."[2] The Lord knows that when we allow ourselves to engage our imagination, whether for good or as in this case for self-promotion, it is an action that has the ability to produce the unexpected. It holds the potential to drive us to more navel-gazing or (the better option) to guide us to a deeper, more personal relationship with the Creator of the universe.

One of the most revealing and transformative things about us is what we are willing to imagine about God; what we secretly picture and suppose God to be. The more we believe that what the Lord reveals about Himself in the Text is true, the more willing we are to imagine where He might guide us today. God invites us into His ingenious plan by asking us to *dare* believe He pursues us, desires to be in relationship with us, and loves us more than we can fathom. He is *daring* us to imagine He is today what He showed Himself to be more than two thousand years ago when He walked this earth in human form.

Admittedly, there are many who portray God as a heavenly being who doesn't care, is light years away, and is just waiting for us to mess up. With suffering at the forefront and injustice rampant, it's hard to believe He exists at all. Some think He is gracious, compassionate, merciful, holy, and relational, but is that how you describe Him? What if you've never experienced Him that way. Would you *dare* imagine Him as your Lord, your Savior, your Redeemer, your Friend? Or is that too much of a stretch?

Tapping into the divine imagination within us builds our faith and leads us into an intimate relationship with God through Jesus Christ. It's a necessary first step toward following the Lord, especially when we possess no tangible evidence that we are headed in the right direction.

Whatever your view is of God, consider this: when we limit our belief of Him, we blind ourselves to what He may want to do in us, through us, and with those around us. He is much more than we can imagine, and His plan for our lives is *never* on our radar. No matter how hard we attempt to design our perfect reality—intensely loved, a great education, a stellar job, a devoted spouse, flawless children, and a happily ever after life—it just doesn't happen that way. We end up living someplace else, bullied at school, betrayed by friends, devastated by illness, and changing our career ten times. Before we realize what happened, destructive decisions have shredded relationships and we find ourselves a single parent. It's unrealistic for anyone to think they can accurately predict the path their life will take, good or bad. As Paul said, "No eye has seen, nor ear heard, nor the heart of man *imagined*, what God has prepared for those who love him."[3]

When we allow our thoughts to correspond with the true being of God, He will impact every faction of our lives. And we will start to recognize how wildly imaginative He is to bring restoration to a lost and dying world by sending Jesus, as God in flesh, to conquer death once and for all. For Jesus spoke to us too when He said to Thomas, "Have you believed because you have seen me? Blessed are those who have not seen and yet have believed."[4]

Believing the Lord will pursue, restore, protect, and instill hope-filled courage—even when disappointment looms—will radically transform the way we walk out our faith and how we engage every person along the way.

I believe the Lord stirs the intellect of our souls to envision something far greater than our current reality, *daring* us to visualize the intangible becoming tangible. Eyes that see the power of love to conquer hate, the inner healing of forgiveness, the miracle of redemption, or the rekindling of a marriage centered on grace. It may have been a metaphorical statement on the condition of our hearts that Jesus restored sight to the blind more often than any other miracle recorded. We are blind, and He wants to give us eyes to see.

I invite you to *dare* engage your divine imagination to believe nothing is impossible with God, that you can ask anything in Jesus name and He will do it for you, that greater things than these will you do, and that He has gone to prepare a place for you.[5] Because when you do, you become empowered to move into your vision.

Vision and Reality

Not long after my word from the Spirit, I unexpectedly found myself with friends, and with Mitch. What an awkward experience as I fought the urge to tell him everything. If God's plan was for us to be together, let's start the ball rolling. (Thankfully, I restrained myself!)

Instead, I recalled God's first word for me that day by the lake: *Relax.* He was telling me that He had it under control. Mitch and I engaged in a superfluous conversation while I said nothing of what I knew and continued to wait. Not too patiently, I must add.

Then one day, I attended a graduation open house and Mitch showed up. Our conversation morphed from high school students to the trials of faith when he suddenly reached into his backpack and handed me his copy of *My Utmost for His Highest* by Oswald Chambers and said, "Take a look at the July 6 entry."

I flipped to that day's devotion and read the title, "Vision and Reality." I was surprised at the heading and even more so at what was written. It started with a Scripture verse from Isaiah 35:7: "And the parched ground shall become a pool."[6] Then Chambers wrote:

> We always have visions, before a thing is made real. When we realize that although the vision is real, it is not real in us, then is the time that Satan comes in with his temptations, and we are apt to say it is no use to go on. Instead of the vision becoming real, there has come the valley of humiliation.
>
> *Life is not as idle ore,*
> *But iron dug from central gloom,*
> *And batter'd by the shocks of doom*
> *To shape and use.*
>
> God gives us the vision, then He takes us down to the valley to batter us into the shape of the vision, and it is in the valley that so many of us faint and give way. Every vision will be made real if we will have patience. Think of the enormous leisure of God! He is never in a hurry. We are always in such a

frantic hurry. In the light of the glory of the vision we go forth to do things, but the vision is not real in us yet; and God has to take us into the valley, and put us through fires and floods to batter us into shape, until we get to the place where He can trust us with the veritable reality. Ever since we had the vision God has been at work, getting us into the shape of the ideal, and over and over again we escape from His hand and try to batter ourselves into our own shape.

The vision is not a castle in the air, but a vision of what God wants you to be. Let Him put you on His wheel and whirl you as He likes, and as sure as God is God and you are you, you will turn out exactly in accordance with the vision. Don't lose heart in the process. If you have ever had the vision of God, you may try as you like to be satisfied on a lower level, but God will never let you.[7]

As I read and reread the devotion that afternoon, my tears fell unnoticed as the Lord brought life to my spirit and encouragement to my soul by the poignant words penned by Chambers. Up to that point, nothing had so clearly depicted what I felt or confirmed what I had been led to imagine. It uniquely illuminated for me that in the spiritual dimension, vision and reality are separated by a significant amount of time, and certain discomfort. And throughout the fulfillment process, the evil one is going to create doubt, try to mess up the plan, and attempt to make us think God is not involved. All the while enticing us to bail on what we believe. Our willingness to *dare* imagine more about God is the first step toward faithfully entering our reality.

Although our God-given vision we hold close to the vest may not be real for us today, by learning to stand on His Word, listen for His whisper, and step forward to follow, our hearts and lives will be forever transformed. Just be assured it's going to look impossible because *daring* to use our imagination, at the beginning, always does.

Chapter 3

A Daring Vision

As an infant, I had a habit of balancing on my stomach along the railing of my crib. Mom would discover me teetering like a gymnast on a two-inch surfboard and frantically snatch me off the rail and place me back on the mattress, only to return minutes later to find me there again. I'm not sure what I was imagining at the time, but it must have been good. Sad to say that even with repeated summers of tumbling class, gymnastics never ended up being my thing (it may have been the tights). I was, however, drawn to basketball.

When my parents made the decision to move across the state for new employment opportunities and leave the home with the dream-filled tree fort, I was hoping I'd find a basketball hoop available for me as before. However, it took a while for Dad to get around to putting one up, which relegated me to settle for punching out the bottom of a wooden bushel basket and nailing it to a backyard oak tree. The rattling sound when the ball went through was mesmerizing, but the idea of playing with a real team on a real court was even more appealing. My only available option was to join an elementary boys' basketball team. I decided to give it a try.

The day of our first game, I was so nervous I nearly got sick. Sitting on the bench I watched my ten-year-old teammates enthusiastically run up and down the court doing their best to make the game look like basketball.

Late in the contest the coach put me in, and within minutes I was fouled. I timidly made my way to the free throw line. The only girl on the court, and not very tall to boot, the official asked if I would like to move a few steps closer to shoot my free throw. Wanting to save face, I declined his offer and stepped up to the line. I bounced the ball twice and launched what felt like a perfect shot, only to watch it fall painfully short. Not only was it short, it wasn't even high enough. The ball dribbled out of bounds without touching a thing. I wanted to crawl off the court.

Success as a fifth-grade baller and the reality of my skills were further apart than what I had envisioned and what I wanted to admit—which was sadly disappointing. But I visualized an aptitude greater than what was apparent and chose to stick with the sport. Something about the game compelled me to spend hours after school and into the night trying new shots and tracking how many I could make in a row.

I continued my love of basketball through junior high and high school, always envisioning that one day I might be an integral player on a team and possibly, if I worked hard enough, earn a scholarship to play in college (if the WNBA existed, I'm sure I would have dreamt of playing there too).

In high school two books encouraged me to develop concrete measures to pursue my vision as a Jesus-follower, and I found they also helped me pursue my vision as an athlete: *I Dare You* by William H. Danforth and *I Love the Word Impossible* by Ann Kiemel. They literally *dared* me to embrace a plan to realize what others believed unfeasible. With the help of gifted coaches and teachers, I set goals and created a plan to attain what I envisioned. That plan involved attending intense camps and workouts, following a fitness regimen, and pushing myself to take my skills to the next level by playing ball with the boys. I demanded a lot of myself, sacrificing both time and a social life. My pursuits weren't always successful, yet I remained persistent. In the meantime, I read more about how God inspired everyday people to pursue unmanifested visions as though real and gained the courage to keep pouring my heart and soul into my own.

Early on in my basketball experience, I discovered that conceiving a vision is a whole lot easier than walking it out (and that a fit body doesn't magically take shape on its own). It was not enough to imagine my future or to have a great strategy to get there, I needed *daring* vision. Soon I saw the need for that same *daring* vision in other areas of my life as well—my academics, my work, my relationships, and especially my view of God. That's when I began to ask the Lord for a life that was unusual, out of the ordinary. I wanted to make a difference. I wanted a *daring* vision that took a different path. A *daring* vision that would enable me to step out to follow the Lord into the unknown and encourage others to do the same. Little by little He began to answer that prayer.

The most *daring* and life-altering vision I ever held was the belief that what the Bible says about God is true and that every promise He made in the Text will come to pass. Since the Bible says, "Greater things than these will you do." [8] I *dared* to believe it. Now it's not *daring* because the Lord might fail to live up to what He says about Himself or fail to fulfill His promises, it's *daring* because few people are willing to embrace that vision. Traveling this road can be lonely and won't feel all that great, which is risky. Are we willing to contend with skeptics that incite us to bail? Are we willing to trust the Lord to be enough when it seems we don't have enough? While this *daring* vision may be considered by some to be one of the most arduous to pursue, it will forever be the most rewarding.

But What Is Vision?

Many of us believe we know what vision is, but too often we confuse it for other things. Vision is more than a daydream or an escape from reality. Vision is what helps us set a course of action that will lead to a desired outcome, whether that be to start on the varsity team as a freshman or to receive an acceptance letter from the college of our choice. When we embrace the vision of a musical career, financial freedom, or even an athletic conquest and then take steps toward its fulfillment, we are empowered to maintain focus and resolve even when we can't see the path ahead. This counters the assumption that vision pertains to our eyesight, because it is possible to have vision and to move forward without seeing a thing. Many thriving corporations and educational institutions hold creative brainstorming sessions to cultivate clearly articulated vision statements that will facilitate achieving long-term goals—even though nothing is visible to the naked eye. We can do it too.

Nurturing our vision helps fill the gap between what our eyes see and what our minds can picture. Truth be told, the vision of our hearts may see more clearly than eyesight testing at 20/20. Our eyes alone limit us. Facts, although true, limit us. It is a fact that up until May 1954, no one had ever run a four-minute mile. No one believed it was humanly possible. And then came Roger Bannister. He had a vision that he could run faster. That vision propelled him to persistently work at what he could not see but what he believed he could achieve. And when he shattered that glass ceiling, not only did his vision become reality, but he also motivated hundreds to cross a seemingly unattainable barrier in rapid succession. Roger pushed forward because of his vision.

A vision (such as raising a family of integrity or creating Disneyland) requires imagination, wisdom, and—most importantly—a strategy to achieve a goal. That strategy may be as simple as speaking truth in every conversation or as complex as outlining an intricate design for a world-famous theme park. The practical ways we move ahead in our visions differ for each of us and depend on what we aspire to.

Regardless of the end goal, our visions generate hope when navigating unfamiliar territory. They grow in us the courage to stay the course and not bail at the first sign of difficulty. For "where there is no vision [no revelation of God and His word], the people are unrestrained; but happy and blessed is he who keeps the law [of God]." [9]

Though vision requires imagination, the two are not synonymous. They are related and they are different. Imagination is the ability to create images in our minds that are not yet real—and may never be. Like being invisible (or in my case being able to dunk). Imagination enhances our vision of something unknowingly possible: picturing travel that exceeds the speed of light, visualizing a world of dazzling creativity, seeing victory before it happens. But it was *daring* vision that enabled Einstein, Disney, and Olympic champions to experience the reality of their dreams.

Daring vision sets forth a plan that requires significant sacrifice coupled with a willingness to assume risk. And it regularly clashes with the view of those content with mediocrity. A *daring* vision stretches you to strive for something few have ever attained. When you assume a *daring* vision, the possibility of disappointing failure is real. But when you commit to a *daring* vision, you find that vision inspires, vision provides passion and purpose, vision enables you to try again and again, vision will change the world and forever alter a life, vision gives you the courage to traverse uncertainty, and vision stirs your heart. And when you make the choice to seek out God's vision for your life, His Spirit empowers you to walk it out.

But How Do We Determine God's Vision for Us?

As a sports camp clinician, I like to invite three volunteers to the front and tell them they are going to race one another. Then with no further direction, I say simply, "Ready? Go!" After a moment of hesitation, one will take off in a full sprint. Another will typically not run at all. And the third will look around to see what the other two are doing and tentatively jog in a different direction. The first person has no vision but is running fast anyway. The second is so fearful of having the wrong vision, they don't go anywhere. And the last person allows the others to dictate where they end up.

Each one may or may not have a vision, but they chose to rely on their own understanding rather than to seek guidance. Unfortunately, we seek God's vision the same way. We take off running without ever asking, listening, or determining God's vision for us. Just about any vision can transform our lives but we really need God's vision not one driven by ego and definitely not God's vision for someone else—even though that may be *really* tempting. I repeatedly fall into that trap. I tend to look left and right (instead of up) to find someone whose life is going in a direction that looks good and adopt their vision as mine.

My problem is, if I'm not following someone else, I'm diving into the deep end way too soon (which like the first runner is just as bad). I remember watching a marathon on television and deciding to go out and run eight miles that afternoon (not smart when you've never run that far in your life—my body ached for days!). While it may have been God's plan for Roger Bannister to break the four-minute mile, it is painfully true that it is not mine and I need to be okay with that. We must choose to follow God's vision for us and be willing to trust what we cannot see will turn out just as He intends.

Sadly, we often chase what we think will make us feel good or grab onto whatever idea might roam through our heads and then hold onto it as though it's the Lord's design for us. To pursue a godly vision, we must discern the difference. For example, just because we can craft the perfect lie, learn to ditch the police, or find the best way to cheat on a test, that doesn't mean it's God's vision or plan. We need to repeatedly ask the Lord for His insight.

To do that, we need to turn to God's Word, which reveals His character and His love for us. When the Word is not our first reference or what we use to direct our decisions, it puts us in danger of relying on the experiences of others or our own feelings to manufacture our vision, which may not be God's vision for us at all. Just because something makes sense doesn't mean it's from God. Just because something feels good, doesn't mean it's God's will. Just because what I hear is what I want to hear doesn't mean God approves.

A colleague once told me, "I feel God calling me into Christian music, to produce multiple albums and travel internationally, even though I'll have to max out all our credit cards to provide for my family."

I am not suggesting all debt is wrong, but we need to trust that if the Lord is guiding us, then we can believe the apostle Paul, who said, "my God will supply every need of yours according to his riches in glory in Christ Jesus." [10]

A man once shared with me, "My wife is a loving person but not a believer. A few months ago, I met another woman who desired to study the Bible and go to church with me. I think the Lord is telling me to leave my wife to be with the other woman who shares my desires and interests."

I am absolutely certain it wasn't the Lord telling him to leave his wife. In the Text (which is the first place to go to hear from God), Jesus said, "Whoever divorces his wife, except for sexual immorality, and marries another, commits adultery." [11] While mitigating circumstances may influence marital decisions in a variety of ways (and these are simple illustrations) we need to go to the Word to hear the Lord's take on what we currently face. In other words, both of those people possessed a vision, but it wasn't God's vision. A realization they might have come to themselves had they first turned to the Scriptures.

We can be confident that God will never contradict His Word. Ever. "God, who never lies … is the same yesterday and today and forever."[12] And His Word is the most important way God speaks to us. When the Word is not our go-to, we can be seduced down a destructive path without even knowing it. Take Saul, king of ancient Israel, who consulted a medium and lost his kingdom; the prophet Jonah who ran from God and ended up in the belly of a great fish; or Sapphira, a believer in the early church, who tried to deceive fellow believers (and the Lord) and she paid with her life.[13]

A favorite passage of mine is Psalm 27:4, which says, "One thing I ask from the Lord, this only do I seek: that I may dwell in the house of the Lord all the days of my life, to gaze upon the beauty of the Lord and to seek him in his temple."[14] When I don't know what direction to go or when I believe I have discerned God's vision for me but don't know how to step out into that vision, I have to remind myself to seek His guidance by reading the Text and spending time in His presence. He needs to become the object of my pursuit.

One of God's visions for us is very clear: to grow deeper in our relationship with Him. When we fix our eyes on Jesus and choose to emulate a lifestyle that pleases Him, He will fill in the missing details. Hear the heart of Jesus in Matthew 6:33: "Seek first the kingdom of God and his righteousness, and all these things will be added to you." Jesus will be faithful to show us what we need to know when we need to know it. The more we aspire to seek Him first, the more our trust in the Lord will grow. And with it, our *daring* vision.

The Word, however, is not the only way God communicates. He uses people, creation, circumstances, peace, music, even a downloaded whisper from His Spirit that bears witness with ours. Rarely does He articulate audacious dreams to sacrifice your child on an altar, to pray for the sun to stop moving, or to head toward a giant with a slingshot.[15]

And seldom does He express Himself audibly. I am sure some people have heard the Lord that way, but I have not met them, and it's never happened to me.

God's vision for each one of us often stems from the passion He puts in our hearts or impresses within our thoughts. But before we rush headlong toward some random inkling, it is important to be sure what we believe is from the Lord. In *Sun Stand Still*, Steven Furtick suggests, "If the dream in your heart isn't biblically based, focused on Jesus, affirmed by the key people in your life, and tethered to your passions, gifts and life experiences, chances are you're way off prompt."[16]

A Risky Proposition

A *daring* vision enables us to start a new job, send our kids to school, pursue a relationship, or step out on stage. But vision involves risk. Success or failure is on the line because not every vision will come to pass no matter how much planning or effort goes into it. The second interview may not happen, the college rejection letter could arrive, you might be cut from the team or given the role of a standby. He may not look your way, she could say no, or you might forget what you were going to say at the worst possible moment. Worse still, the direction of your life could be shifted forever by what you choose to believe about God.

I want to *dare* envision the impossible—like marrying Mitch or playing ball with the boys—yet it is a real temptation to play it safe and not risk the heartache. Because, while imagination may help create a vision worth pursuing, by itself, it doesn't guarantee success. When you *dare* to take a stand in faith and go after a vision, failure is an option.

In the 1950s, Florence Chadwick was one of the most dominant distance swimmers, men or women. She swam the English Channel three times, shattering previous records. But it was during a swim from Catalina Island, twenty-one miles off the coast of California, where she faced one of her most difficult challenges. A pre-dawn start found Florence swimming through thick fog, pounding waves, and shivering cold temperatures in her attempt to reach the coastline. After fifteen hours, she was exhausted and wanted to stop. Alongside in a boat, both her trainer and coach implored her to keep swimming; she was almost there. Obscured by fog and surf the land was indistinguishable and, finally, Florence felt she could no longer continue and chose to end the swim. As they reluctantly brought her into the boat and headed for shore, she saw they were only a half-mile from land.

When later interviewed, Florence had no excuses for her exhaustion, but responded if she could have seen the land, she would have been able to finish.[17] Being able to see what she was aiming for may have helped Florence complete the swim that day, but she remained committed to her vision, and months later reached her goal.

God-given vision involves developing steps to progress toward what He is leading us to picture. Florence had a plan to attain her vision, and we need one too, even when our vision is a deeper relationship with Jesus. God-given visions produce courage, purpose, unexpected results, and the ability to dust ourselves off and try again. Frustration and disappointment are inescapable but having vision helps us navigate uncertainty. Without it, we are prone to give up too quickly or bail out of fear.

It was a stormy night on the Sea of Galilee as Jesus' disciples frantically tried to get their boat safely to shore. Fear gripped their souls when they spotted Jesus walking toward them on the water. As Jesus encouraged Peter to step out of the boat and come to Him, the vision He had for Peter was not to walk on water. The goal was simply to join Him. Peter stepped out of the boat and onto the water and started walking toward Jesus, but fear caused him to go under. He didn't begin to sink because he could no longer see Jesus, Peter began to sink because his doubt clouded his vision. He no longer believed drawing near to Jesus was possible. Jesus didn't lose faith in Peter, and Peter didn't lose faith in Jesus; Peter lost the vision of relationship.[18]

God uniquely designed a plan for Peter and for us. A vision and purpose that only we can fulfill. And that vision has been in place long before we were.[19] When our lives go away from His plan—because we are running aimlessly or following someone who has no idea where they are going—God isn't at fault we are. But even if we have separated ourselves from those who follow Jesus, haven't opened our Bible in years (the physical one or an app), and aren't sure the Lord cares about us anyway, by turning toward Jesus again or for the first time, the Lord is fully capable of fulfilling His desire for our lives. My linear mind has difficulty comprehending how that is possible, but with God everything is.[20]

Dare to believe that as you "delight yourself also in the Lord ... He will give you the desires of your heart."[21] Maybe this implies when we truly delight ourselves in Him, our own desires will be fulfilled. But I often wonder if the verse means that when we find joy by choosing to follow Jesus or as we chase after His instruction found in the Text or when we look for His presence in our lives, He will then place *His* desires in our hearts? You know, a vision. Maybe even a *daring* vision. Something stirring in our souls, begging us to break through our apprehension and seek Him as though we are seeking air to breathe. It could involve bringing a meal to the new neighbors down the street, joining a prison ministry, sharing your story, or mentoring a troubled teen. People of *daring* vision accept they are gifted for a purpose and become willing to walk in that giftedness even when it's scary, even if it's risky, even when it seems insignificant, and even when failure feels inevitable. People of vision *dare* to choose to look beyond themselves and their circumstances.

In what area has God gifted you? What is it you are passionate about? Is there affirmation from key people in your life for the *daring* vision that may be stirring in your soul? Will the pursuit of this vision draw you closer to the Lord whether or not it is viewed as successful?

Stepping Out in My Vision

I was now at another crossroad. It had been over a month and fear had kept me from divulging to anyone what I had experienced. Would I *dare* believe the Lord placed a vision in my heart about Mitch enough to tell someone? Or would I disregard what I heard, do what feels good, refrain from ruffling any proverbial religious feathers, and keep my reputation intact?

The people most gifted to provide me with wise counsel and who understood the challenge to walk out a godly vision were my parents—especially Mom. Whenever I grappled with the Text and was tempted to limit my view of God, her steady wisdom and rock-solid faith helped me refocus on truth. I finally decided to drive the five miles to their house and reveal what I believed I heard from the Lord regarding Mitch. As I walked into the living room and sat with her on the same inviting couch where we used to kneel and pray as a family, I shared with her my feelings of rejection over the recent breakup, what I believed I heard the Spirit impress to me, and my ensuing unbelief. I poured out my fears, my insecurities, and my overwhelming doubt that hearing the Lord this way could be a real thing.

Mom listened patiently and smiled. After a pensive pause, she said, "Praise the Lord, you are gaining discernment." Her encouragement, her embrace, and her prayers felt like fresh water to my parched soul. Tears of renewed faith rolled down my face. Her gracious and loving reply infused me with the passion to step forward into the Lord's vision. I had no idea how much I needed her support. Soon I shared my story with two close friends. Although unfamiliar with anything comparable, they also affirmed my experience and prayed for me.

Choosing to live out what I said I believed and reengaging my heart in what felt impractical was entirely foreign. My default was knowing how to "do church" and make myself look good. Even though the Spirit's words felt out of the ordinary, the stories of *daring* men and women throughout the Text—who also chose to walk toward what they couldn't see—emboldened me. I broke through my fear and stepped out to follow the Lord when it didn't make sense (a daily choice that became a vital necessity). With no idea where I was headed or if I was prepared for the journey, I *dared* to unlock my calculated heart and allow the tender voice of the Lord to settle in, even if I missed the mark. Trusting that if I missed Him, He would find me.

My vision from the Lord involved significant risk. But I wanted to be a woman of *daring* faith, to do something extraordinary with and for God. Are you ready to step out with the Lord into the unknown and embrace His vision for your life? Together we can *dare* choose to follow God and trust He will provide, even while knowing obstacles lie ahead. Let's believe that as we cling to His Word, our spirits will be fortified with hope as we move forward into God's *daring* vision with adventurous faith.

Chapter 4

THE GREAT ADVENTURE

I've never been one to gravitate toward pursuits such as cliff jumping or swimming with sharks; white water rafting or hiking a new trail is more my idea of an adventure. It might be that you find Black Friday shopping or a culinary test plenty of exhilaration for you. But whatever your preference, an invigorating adventure usually involves a perceived element of danger or uncertainty (like a race down the aisle for discounted earbuds or an intense fear the crème brûlée will never set).

The unknown—while thrilling for adrenaline junkies—creates unwanted tension and paralyzing anxiety in many others. And while you may be compulsively drawn to the excitement of an adventure, it's miserable to discover you have been unwillingly thrown into one. I would much rather choose my adventure and level of risk.

Yet as much as we try to control our surroundings, unexpected and problematic diversions are inescapable and make us feel hurled off course. You know what I mean. We plan for a long-awaited getaway and illness strikes; we try to start a family and pregnancy eludes us; we prepare to enjoy the peace and quiet of an empty nest and our parents move in. With little warning an abrupt detour forces us down an alternate route. Without patience, a creative imagination, and an infusion of God's power, a sudden precarious event can be heart-wrenching and leave us discouraged.

During my senior year of high school, I encountered just that. Through a series of poor teenage decisions, I ended up flipping our family car off the side of the road. Suffice it to say at seventeen, I wasn't entirely proficient behind the wheel. While no automobile mishap is ever good, even more disastrous for me was that the accident occurred just hours before our first softball game of the spring season.

Lying on the gurney in the emergency room, dreams of a glowing finish to my final season faded fast. X-rays revealed a broken left wrist, which likewise shattered my hopes. *Lord, what am I supposed to do now?* I prayed. *My senior year can't end like this.* I fought back a flood of tears. For a softball player a broken wrist is a serious roadblock.

Some may consider playing sports trivial and certainly not a matter of life and death. However, for the impassioned athlete the resulting joy or pain is very real. As I mourned everything I would lose once they casted my wrist, my mind wandered to a paper I wrote in middle school on Pete Gray, a one-armed Major League Baseball (MLB) out-fielder for St. Louis in 1945. (Clearly a divine intervention ... no way I'm smart enough to recall that assignment.) I started to wonder if there was a way to salvage my softball season. Could I possibly play ball with one hand, as Pete had? No one I knew ever tried it before, and 1945 was a long time ago. The fact I played second base—which required ample fielding and quick reactions—made the whole idea more problematic than if I played in the outfield.

With the end to my season a near foregone conclusion, I was eager to attempt whatever might get me back on the field with my teammates. Initially, the thought of playing softball with a broken wrist seemed crazy but the Lord kept stirring in my spirit faith for an adventure.

My parents were less than thrilled at the idea of me swinging a bat, fielding balls, and running bases with a cast. Even my coach was skeptical. Friends told me I should simply hang up my cleats and forget about playing. But two of my teammates *dared* to view my roadblock from a fresh perspective and the next afternoon joined me on the ball field with a new glove. This time for my right hand.

After many unsuccessful yet creative attempts at fielding one-handed, we finally found something that worked. I would field a grounder, toss the ball less than a foot in the air, shake the glove off, catch the ball with my now bare hand, and make the play (it went to another level when I needed to turn two!). Jim Abbott, the one-armed MLB pitcher for multiple teams in the 1990s, highlighted a similar process.[22] To the surprise of many (including myself), I returned to the softball diamond four days later to play in our next game. Although it required a steep learning curve to play well (and to bat with one hand), the once-threatening detour morphed into an opportunity for a rather adventurous spring. And it all started by *daring* to consider God's perspective, developing a strategy to get there, and believing He would empower me along the way.

A willingness to imagine and to design a plan for what we envision is vital, yet it's not enough. We also need to rely on the Lord to lead us through what may be an unfamiliar and often difficult path. *Daring* in faith to trust the Lord when it's hard and not trust our own giftedness, allows Him to guide us into what might very well turn into a great adventure.

God's Power Displayed

A declaration of faith is really an expression of complete confidence in something or someone, and it's not limited to God. We regularly assume a chair will hold us, the lights will come on when we flip the switch, or that the young guy in the cockpit has been flying for more than fifteen minutes. Yet the faith I invite you to embrace, not only believes God is who He says He is, it is evidenced by what we do. It's more than a mental assent to a belief or a bumper sticker on our car. It's more than an intellectual exercise. Faith expects to see God at work in both our good and bad adventures, not because our faith is some sort of magic trick that conjures Him up, but because He is already there to begin with. Faith helps us recognize the presence and work of the Lord (in our past and in our future) even when we can't physically see a thing. And faith, as necessary to our lives as our hearts, pumps hope into our spirits like it's circulating blood.

My parents lived out a *daring* faith—the kind that regularly anticipated the Lord to move. Just weeks after the conclusion of my adventurous softball season, Dad led a group of teenagers at church through a study that exposed how dabbling in the occult leads to demonic strongholds. Although an unusual topic, stories in the Text of Jesus vanquishing demons, along with compelling individual testimonies of freedom, revealed an astonishing power of the Holy Spirit to defeat evil.

While that subject matter is *daring* for any pastor to assume, my parents never anticipated the intense spiritual attack unleashed in our home the night following that first meeting. Suffice it to say, I witnessed a manifestation of evil unexpectedly revealed in a young man attending the study who had been bound by the chains of the evil one. For the first time our entire family experienced the supernatural power and authority of Jesus Christ as He broke the hold of sin that ravaged this man's life. Watching the spiritual victory unfold before our eyes, I realized God was infinitely more powerful than I ever imagined. And *daring* to follow Him would necessitate embracing an adventure that was uncommon, precarious, and rejected by many in the church.

My parents' willingness to walk an unbeaten path to overcome the dominion of darkness transformed me. I learned that by faithfully standing for what we believe, we tap into the authority available to us as followers of Jesus Christ. And that the Word of God (described as a sword in Ephesians 6) is an invincible weapon in a spiritual battle. My trust in the Lord grew exponentially by seeing God's power displayed. As my parents *dared* to believe that the Lord offered hope and freedom to those under the enemy's control, they stepped into a new adventure. And it became the greatest and most challenging adventure of their lives. Their choice to follow Jesus into uncharted and risky territory ignited in me the confidence to do the same.[23]

Up until that summer, what I had heard in various church circles shaped my teenage perception of God—that the miracles, healings, and supernatural manifestations of the Lord revealed throughout the Text, were not for us today. This confined God to a neatly controlled package and limited His influence in my life. Although not true or comforting, I assumed the Lord watched from a distance so He could catch me when I messed up. If I wanted to stay out of trouble, I just needed to believe Jesus paid the price for my sins and do more things right than I did wrong. I had no idea the Lord wanted a relationship with me.

Following that astounding spiritual victory, my paradigm on faith and what I believed about God began to shift. I started to see the Lord as exceedingly more potent and present than I imagined. And by pursuing relationship with Him, that action *alone* will result in a heart transformation nothing else on our part can ever accomplish. Growing an intimate connection with the Lord changes our view of an apparent roadblock or a sudden adventure. Every unexpected failure, loss, or disappointment now becomes an avenue to deepen our bond with Him rather than a problem. And it opens the door for the mighty presence of the Holy Spirit to drastically alter our reality.

Battling Doubt

Knowing the Lord will reveal Himself through His Word and through a deepening connection with Him, infuses us with courage, increases our trust in Him, and opens our eyes to see what He is already doing around us. But that doesn't stop distracting obstacles from attempting to detour our faith and create doubt.

While trying to live out my faith as a collegiate athlete, I became a desired target for a barrage of the enemies lies. Repeated notions entered my head that God wasn't interested in me so I shouldn't bother talking with Him. When I played poorly, thoughts ransacked my mind to quit. When roommates became contentious, I wanted to find new ones. And when I failed to meet other people's expectations (or my own), frustration set in, and I blamed God. The evil one expended a lot of effort to get me to doubt my purpose on this earth by tempting me to bail on what I said I believed.

But a spark of faith remained lit deep in my spirit … and it's there in yours too. It's what Romans 12:3 describes as, *"the measure of faith that God has assigned."* Unbeknownst to me, the boatload of faith and vision the Lord had poured into my soul was beginning to catch fire. As I *dared* to consider the Creator of the universe wanted a personal relationship with me, I asked for help to see what others didn't and to accept what the Bible said as true (even if it didn't appear that way at the time). And the Lord answered that prayer. Even though my passion still defaulted to sport, I soon found myself expecting to see His hand move in other areas. Sorry to say, my increased faith in God didn't put an end to embarrassing and flawed athletic or musical performances, eliminate failures in the classroom, or fix disappointing friendships. Nevertheless, I began to seek a growing connection with the Lord with the same fervor I poured into a game.

During my final year at university, a high school in my hometown offered me a teaching position which included coaching the varsity basketball team and assisting at the local college. So, within months after playing on nationally ranked university teams (led by *amazing* teammates and coaches), my focus turned to teaching and coaching, determined to continue the success. And I did. Within two years (at twenty-three years old), the college hired me as their head basketball coach. I continued to teach math to teenagers, grew more impassioned by music, and competed internationally with various athletic ministries during the summer months. I was living my dream!

But four years into pursuing success in all areas of my life—teaching, music, coaching, and dating—they fired me from my coaching job. The college administrators responsible for making the coaching change reneged on our deal. (The position would remain mine if we were winning and I worked to complete my master's degree. True and true.) This stunning turn of events rocked my world.

Like a freak perfect storm, people I considered friends had no idea how to console my wounded heart and started to pull away. I felt abandoned, visionless, and vulnerable. My identity had been in athletic success and relationships, and I lost both. The humiliation kept me from wanting to be seen around town, convinced people loved me only for my accomplishments not for who I was. I faced what appeared to be an insurmountable roadblock and saw no way out of the pain.

To make matters worse, pursuing my goal of marriage in the wild world of dating, resulted in nothing more than full weekends and broken hearts. Specifically, mine. Repeatedly mine. Frustration mounted as love eluded me.

My great adventure had spun out of control.

Now thrown on what felt like a dark and precarious side road, I labored to follow Jesus. Being fired never crossed my radar. The thought of being thirty and still single never did either. I believed I controlled more of my life than I did and consistently pushed back on the verse "I can do nothing on my own."[24] My brilliant plan for life included Jesus but I was following Him to get where *I* wanted to go instead of following Jesus to get where *He* wanted me to go. I treated Him as the small emergency tire you put on your car when you're in trouble and not the person behind the steering wheel. Now yanked from the driver's seat I watched my world crumble. I had no idea where I was headed. Once a master manipulator of situations (and I'm ashamed to say even people) to get where I wanted to go, I was now lost and out of gas. Abandoned and helpless, my life was in chaos. I frantically searched for anything to help me get out of this funk.

Creating Space for the Lord

While trying to navigate the roadblocks of being fired and still single, my pastor gave me a book of short stories titled, *God Guides,* written by Mary Geegh, a missionary to India. In it she illustrated her process of active, listening prayer. The idea of pausing to hear the voice of the Lord and following what He said was foreign to me. I thought prayer meant I talked to God, and *He* listened (and of course complied), not the other way around. The intimacy of her relationship with the Lord intrigued me. Could it be that the Lord wants to make Himself known in ways I have not yet experienced? Could it be He has a better plan for my life and relationships than I do?

In the Text it says Moses saw the Lord face to face,[25] and that Jesus Christ is the same yesterday, today, and forever.[26] If the Bible is true, then shouldn't I *dare* believe the Lord still desires to reveal Himself to us today?

As I read through the older Testament, I noticed the phrase *says the Lord* kept showing up. God seems to be depicted as talking to people all the time. (It was many years later when using a computer word search program, that I discovered "says the Lord" occurs 495 times in the ESV translation—not including derivatives like, "the Lord said" or "God said," which would add hundreds more!) So, I resolved to believe

God wanted to talk with me too. Perhaps He had something to say about my job, my relationships, and even my aching heart. I decided to operate under the assumption that when I listen for His direction, He just might give me ears to hear.

Consequently, I began to create space to hear the Lord by reading the Word and quieting my spirit to listen for His voice. In a journal I wrote praises to the Lord for who He was, confessed ways I failed Him, asked Him to intervene, and made a gratitude list. My prayer life turned into intentional and relational conversations, transforming rote phrases void of feeling into honest expressions of pain and hope.

Tracking my prayers (and the Lord's answers) shed light on His faithfulness. And through journaling I became better able to focus, recognize truth, fight negativity, and clearly express my thoughts to the Lord. As I learned to listen, a deeper relationship emerged.

Up until that time, conversations with the Lord mirrored how I communicated with others; it was one way and centered on me. My words, my demands, my opinions, and my thoughts as to what God (or friends) should do next. I had treated Him like a supernatural vending machine existing solely to meet my needs. But the Lord wanted to share His heart too. And just as in any good relationship, for that to happen I needed to stop talking and actively listen.

I started to dialogue *with* Him and listen for what He wanted to say. And in those quiet moments when the Holy Spirit spoke, I wrote what my spirit heard. Sometimes I would ask specific questions and wait for a response. Choosing to believe John 16:13, that "When the Spirit of the truth comes, he will guide you into all the truth, for he will not speak on his own authority, but whatever he hears he will speak, and he will declare to you the things that are to come."

Author Marcus Warner describes listening for the Spirit in his book, *Understanding the Wounded Heart*: "For the first time, it hit me that God's voice comes to me as thoughts in my head. It was really a matter of learning to discern which thoughts were from Him."[27] God has unmistakably spoken to my spirit through His, and although I have never heard an audible voice, He still communicates.

When I first started listening for the Lord's voice, I feared He would grasp the opportunity to bring up all the ways I messed up in the past, tell me something I really didn't want to hear, or ultimately reject me as woefully inadequate, but it never happened. Without fail, the Spirit deposited precious words into my soul. *I love you. I am proud of you. Stay in the race. Pursue Me. Don't give up. I am faithful and I am enough. Your heart is in My hands. You make Me smile.*

By listening for the Lord and mining His Word, I became better able to handle the disappointment of being fired, the loss of control, and the evil one's lies that I would never amount to anything. Over time I discovered that memorizing and meditating on God's truth destroys the fabrications of the enemy that threaten defeat. "No weapon that is fashioned against you shall succeed"[28] doesn't mean that no weapon will be formed against us, but rather, when we firmly stand on truth, the Holy Spirit will embolden us to walk through each adventure—no matter how sudden or difficult—and to follow God's vision for our lives. By choosing to believe God wants to speak to us and that we can learn to hear His voice, we draw closer to His heart.

The biggest obstacle to hearing from the Lord is continuing to believe He wants to speak to us and that He will. We must first expect the Lord to speak before we will ever hear His downloaded whisper into our spirit. As mentioned before, it is what we believe about God that will ultimately transform us. Will we *dare* to create space to hear Him? Will we *dare* listen for the Lord to speak? Will we *dare* believe the Text that says when we are still, we will know that He is God?[29]

Hearing from the Lord, although not as strange as it sounds, requires a posture of active listening. His voice may be no more than a check in our spirit that tells us to smile at our neighbors, to help those in need, to speak the truth in love, to respect our spouse, or to serve in children's ministry. We often hear from the Lord and may even know what He desires. The question is will we *dare* follow the knowing in our hearts?

Creating in our spirit a place where the Lord can regularly speak to us is one way we can "pray without ceasing."[30] And once we listen *for* Him, then we must choose whether we will listen *to* Him. Yes, a great adventure involves imagination and vision, and it absolutely takes faith: the substance God uses to cultivate courage to stay the course amid disappointment. Because while a great adventure sounds exciting, it is difficult to navigate well. We need faith in the Lord to *dare* believe He wants to be involved in our lives, and to help move us through roadblocks and repeated failures.

Listening to the Lord Leads to *Daring* Faith

After losing my job, I struggled to listen for His voice. Weary and beaten down, my confidence waned. Wisdom, once described to me as a hearing heart, seemed elusive. Yet through the frustration I resolved to view God as wanting to be in relationship with me and stepped out in faith; at times blindly ignoring what I saw and how I felt. And in my quest to *dare* hear Him speak, my eyes and ears were opened in surprising ways.

Late one night, friends from out of town dropped by for the weekend. I had volunteered to help with an elementary basketball clinic the following morning and lamented the timing. Wanting to honor my commitment, I left early for the gym. As I drove and talked with the Lord, I sensed the Holy Spirit impress on my heart to turn around and go back. That didn't sound right so I kept driving. I felt the prompting again. This time I argued the logic of that choice and continued. Once more the Spirit urged me to turn around. This time I paused.

If I am trying to hear His voice, and this is the Lord, I should probably obey. Though His prompting made no sense, I *dared* to appear irresponsible and be a no-show for the clinic so I could follow the Lord.

I hesitantly drove back and spent the day with friends and family, though I continued to feel unsettled that I backed out of something I said I would do. I called the coach the next day to apologize for missing the clinic. Before I said anything, she blurted out, "You didn't show up Saturday, did you? I forgot to call. The clinic was canceled."

Listening to God in something so small made me want to listen for even bigger things! And God gave me that opportunity, because soon afterwards the Lord spoke to me the phrase I'll never forget, *"Relax. You're to marry Mitch Carver. And it's going to look impossible."*

A few months after hearing those words—and still wondering what exactly I was supposed to do with them—I attended a professional golf event to encourage my friend Jayne who was playing. In the fourth and final round of the tournament, Jayne was on the thirteenth hole, three shots off the lead. A golf course is a calm and serene place to talk with the Lord (if you're not playing), and in that conversation, I heard the Spirit say, *"She is going to win, but she doesn't need to know."*

What?

Jayne teed off on the par 3 and airmailed the green. The ball ended up at the base of an embankment, surrounded by mud from rain the night before.

Now I know I didn't hear right.

She stepped up to the ball and knocked it on the green, leaving herself a twenty-foot, double breaking putt. As I watched the ball drop into the hole for par, my heart started to pound. I held my tongue.

Over the next few holes, the leaders stumbled, and Jayne closed the gap. They were tied as she stepped up to the seventeenth tee. When Jayne made birdie (taking one less shot than necessary on that hole, which is great in golf), I nearly hyperventilated! She was now leading the tournament. Behind the ropes on the eighteenth hole, I watched her hit the ball to ten feet and sink another birdie putt. Jayne won the tournament by two strokes.

It wasn't the stunning victory that elicited in me an incredible wave of emotion (although it was incredibly thrilling!), it was realizing the voice I heard on the golf course was the same voice that planted words in my spirit about Mitch. God was giving me a window into His heart. My confidence to hear God's voice strengthened my resolve to continue stepping out even when I couldn't see. I *dared* to trust Him with my great adventure, no matter what I faced along the way.

It takes courage to walk beside me on this journey. I bless God for those, like my friend Lyn, who have stood the test of time and showed me how *daring* to believe in an extraordinary Jesus will gift us with more. Not more money, more success, or more stuff. Rather more revelation, more wisdom, more courage, more peace . . . more of Him.

Lyn recently told me of a trip her family (three college-age boys and her husband) took to the Virgin Islands. The first day at the resort it rained. Cooped up in a hotel room wasn't their idea of a good time. Lyn prayed for God to stop the rain.

Clouds moved in and the storm continued into the second day. Out on the balcony Lyn was very honest with God (a trait I admire.) "God, why did You fly us all the way down here to spend time in a hotel? Don't You know it took a lot to get us all in the same place? I am not happy with the weather You planned for our weekend away." Lyn paused, and being familiar with listening prayer and the Spirit's still small voice, she waited.

"*Speak to the storm,*" she heard the Lord tell her.

"But, Lord," she responded, "I have been praying for the past two days that the rain would stop, that You would intervene, that You would bind up the principalities and powers causing this storm. What else can I do?"

"*Speak to the storm.*"

"I told You I've been praying for You to step in and stop the rain!"

"*Speak to the storm.*"

It clicked. She decided to take authority over the storm from her position as a believer and follower of Christ.

"In the name of Jesus and by His power, storm you have to cease. You have no right to be here, and by the power given me through of the blood of Jesus Christ, I command you to go. Storm, you need to leave this place now."

Nothing happened immediately, and Lyn remained on the balcony discouraged. Then the clouds began to split, slowly creating a small window over their resort. The sun came out and everything changed, including Lyn's spirit and faith. She praised God and confessed her doubt. The clouds stayed off to the side, and for the rest of their time in St. Thomas, the weather was beautiful.

I'm not claiming we can control the elements on a whim, but my spirit is inspired by Lyn's willingness to listen and to act in faith. Maybe you find yourself on the verge of stepping out into your own great adventure, or you have been reluctantly shoved into one. Embracing a fresh perspective and discovering ways to encounter Jesus opens you up to incredible possibilities. For in the renewing of our minds, our lives will be transformed. (Romans 12:2) Choose to be forever changed by *daring* in faith to act on what we say we believe. Take a risk. Listen for God's voice. Then follow. And as we courageously step out and listen for God to speak—confident He desires an intimate relationship with each of us—we will grow to know His heart and begin to grasp the tremendous power He offers us to break through whatever threatens to derail His call on our lives.

Let our great adventure with Him begin.

Chapter 5

THE UNDERDOG

Two years passed by, and Mitch had yet to express an interest in me. Frustration mounted as weekends dawdled along like a bad movie. Well-meaning people would ask if I was seeing anyone, and I had nothing to say. Students peppered me with, "Why aren't you married? Do you have a boyfriend? Don't you want children?" and the ever-present, "You know, I have an uncle . . . " Since some of the students knew Mitch, my comeback was rarely more than a smile.

To keep my mind off what wasn't happening with Mitch (and the fact I was now in my mid-thirties), when I wasn't teaching, I served with a variety of ministry organizations around the world as an athlete, chaplain, vocalist, conference speaker, and coach. Yet even there I failed to escape well-meaning mothers, sisters, and friends who produced many "eligible" men to help me "settle down." Their intentions were kind, but it made finding a reason to say no to potential suitors awkward.

A couple of years earlier, when I first shared with Mom what I believed the Lord had imparted to my spirit about Mitch, her words breathed welcomed life into my dubious soul. Now discouraged by the apparent lack of progress (and the disappointment of having to turn down potential dates), I sought her out again. In the middle of our conversation about how to overcome challenges in the classroom (she was an educator too), I abruptly asked, "Do you think it would be all right for me to date while I wait?"

Sensing my exasperation, she paused. Her simple and gentle response was profound. "The Lord will let you know. Ask Him."

Yeah, I probably should have started there. It wasn't as if I was looking for somebody else to marry, I just wanted a guy to go out with on occasion. (There's something inherently wrong with that logic.) When I finally proposed to the Lord my brilliant idea, His Spirit calmly impressed upon mine, *You can date if you want, but what's the point?*

Right.

My tendency as a little girl was to follow the rules and to do the right thing. So as an adult, when Dad and Mom offered their opinions and concluded with, "But the choice is up to you," my decision was simple: I would honor them by following their advice. And I chose to honor the Lord here too.

Occasionally a male friend would volunteer to escort me to a special event, but God kept the door closed for me to become invested in dating. My response to relationship queries soon became, "I trust the Lord's plan." While the words may have been easy to say, they took years to settle into my soul. I felt perpetually single. Surely people wondered what was wrong with me. I know I did.

It is a struggle to choose to follow a path that goes against what everyone understands to be conventional. And some paths are unorthodox for a reason: past efforts of many brave visionaries haven't ended well. But the longing to be part of a one-off success story drives a select few to forge ahead. In *daring* to step out into the unfamiliar, I knew I needed to expect to encounter failure en route to the Lord's vision. The appearance (or reality) of failure shouldn't come as a surprise. In my case, the vision was to marry Mitch—and it didn't look promising.

The Failure Option

Shortly after my conversation with Mom, a friend invited me to enter a 5K road race. Never a fan of running, 3.1 miles seemed about 3 miles too long. However, the athlete in me found it difficult to turn down a challenge, so I signed up. My commitment to run came paired with a desire to perform well. This drove me to train throughout the week and to purchase new shoes and running attire. If I wasn't going to finish at the front of the pack, I would at least look good.

As we stood on the picturesque shore of Lake Michigan, the race marshal explained the route to hundreds of eager faces. What my friend neglected to mention was half the race was up hill! Having trained on level ground, my legs were spent after the first mile. I had to force myself to turn around at the midway point and head back up the hill from the other side. When a seventy-year-old woman with braids to her waist and a guy dribbling two basketballs passed me on the back stretch, I was mortified. It took years before I *dared* enter another race.

No one enjoys the humbling aspect of failure. And the experience is unavoidable. My failures—whether they were forgetting song lyrics on television, missing free throws to lose a big game, experiencing multiple breakups, or having the announcement of my firing make the front page of the newspaper—produced a crushing weight on my heart. Picking myself back up to try again felt like an insurmountable task.

I sensed something similar while waiting for Mitch. Although he had no idea what I had heard from the Lord, the simple fact that he wasn't pursuing a relationship with me was painful and hard not to take as a personal failure.

When I face the potential of an undesirable outcome, I want to do something to prevent it from happening. Train harder, work harder, try harder, pray harder. Just do something! Fearful and impatient, I attempted to jumpstart the relationship. If I knew Mitch would be at an event, I creatively found a way to be present hoping he would notice me. I sent him random cards of encouragement and emails that contained information on his favorite hobbies. On his birthday I gave him a gift. My goal wasn't to mess up God's plan, I just thought He needed my help to move it along. Unfortunately, my botched efforts to accelerate things created even greater angst when Mitch didn't get it. The more time passed, the more I felt like a failure. It was excruciating.

When we experience recurrent failure, we wind up being perceived as an underdog: people no one expects anything of. It can be demoralizing when those we know (and those we don't) express doubt that we will ever accomplish something meritorious. The redeeming aspect of failure is that we have the choice to sing another song, take the shot again, go on a second date, apply for a new job, and enter a different race (one void of hills and a headwind off the lake). And in that one shining moment when an underdog pulls the upset and defies the odds, it's mesmerizing.

My nephew Phil was ten years old when he entered a car in a Pinewood Derby race. These remarkable events pair a young person with an adult, and together over the course of a few weeks, they create a car out of a small block of wood and four plastic wheels that will roll down a thirty-two-foot wooden track. Phil and his dad spent hours designing, whittling, sanding, and painting his car all in preparation for the big race. On the day of the competition, a youthful exuberance filled the air. Phil was one of the first to race. He nervously placed his car in the starting block next to his opponent and stepped off to the side. Within seconds the gate went up and the two cars sped down the track.

But Phil's car never made it to the finish line. Twice Phil watched his car travel ten feet and stop. His quivering lower lip showed his heartbreak. He had been so excited for this day. Now he was the underdog.

Two men graciously took his car off to the side and fiddled with the wheels. A few moments later they placed the car back at the starting line. The gate lifted and the two cars took off down the track again. To everyone's surprise Phil's car not only completed the race, it finished first. Four more races ensued, and his car won them all. In a daze, Phil walked away with the first-place trophy! After such a hopeless start, no one saw this upset coming.

How many times have we lost faith after seeing our first few attempts not even begin to resemble our dreams? How many times have we bailed when we couldn't see a way out? Humiliation from inevitable setbacks doesn't mean that our pursuit of God's vision is futile or that we have somehow missed the plan He has for our lives. It is absolutely possible to remain faithful when voices of doubt and rejection threaten to douse the hopeful flame of those of us who *dare* risk. And the power for us to do so comes from the Holy Spirit. Through His strength, I was able to hold onto the belief that I was to marry Mitch, with the hope that my persistence through anticipated failure might just lead to a stunning outcome.

We Are Not Done

Ten minutes remained in the 1990 NCAA Division III Women's Basketball National Championship game between Hope College from West Michigan and St. John Fisher College from Upstate New York. The sentimental favorite, Hope, had battled hard but found themselves behind by twenty points. Fans were resigning themselves to the reality that their hometown team was going down in defeat. Their resilience to get this far was impressive, but watching from the stands, failure seemed certain.

And then the implausible happened.

In the next five minutes, the home team cut the lead to ten. Then with three minutes left on the clock, they were down five. An offensive put back and a clutch three-pointer tied the game with less than twenty seconds remaining. The local fans erupted. The rapid evaporation of a twenty-point lead shook the opposition. Frantically, the visitors from New York brought the ball up the court. Their apprehension triggered an unexpected turnover, leaving Hope just five seconds to cover the length of the floor and score.

Time out.

A long pass and a *daring* loose ball scramble produced a foul that put the home team's best free throw shooter at the line. Just over a second remained in the game. Two free throws later, the Hope College women's basketball team came away with their first National Championship appropriately penned, *The Miracle on 8th Street*.

In a gym where I had previously coached the same players a year before, I witnessed a most astonishing comeback, only this time from the stands and not the bench. They pulled off a stunning upset because the players envisioned that a win was possible despite the fact they were a flailing underdog for a good part of the contest. What they believed changed everything. It's the same for us. What we believe has the power to change our life and dream outcomes. If we believe we can thrive and we rely on the Lord's guiding presence, He emboldens us with the power of courage to stay in the fight when others clamor for us to throw in the towel. It puts the possibility of a positive outcome back on the table.

Many people do their best to discourage the ingenuity and creativity of people who are willing to risk failure. When I read the stories of *daring* people, like Thomas Edison, Sidney Poitier, Lucille Ball, Walt Disney, and Vera Wang, who chose to ignore the voice of cynics and their own repeated failures to achieve what everyone thought unattainable, they inspire me to keep going even when victory is doubtful.[31] When we first choose to follow God, it may appear to be a great adventure until the path leads us away from the expected outcome, and suddenly we find ourselves the underdog, wondering where God is in all of this mess and if we heard Him correctly.

Consider what God said to these biblical characters:

Noah, build a boat to save your family.
Abraham, you will father many nations.
Moses, deliver My people.
Daniel, you will rule in Babylon.
Mary, give birth to and raise the Messiah.
Paul, you will bring the gospel to the nations.

God gave each person a coveted assignment, and in between their vision and its fulfillment, they all experienced at least one devastating underdog event that threatened to derail everything:

Noah, your friends and neighbors will mock you.
Abraham, sacrifice your only son.
Moses, you will lead a rebellious people.
Daniel, your faithfulness will land you in a lion's den.
Mary, you will watch your Son be hated and crucified.
Paul, you will be beaten, imprisoned, and left for dead.

The Lord rarely fills us in on the details of what it will mean to heed His voice, nor does He eliminate obstacles along the way. But as we *dare* in faith to walk forward with a persuasive (and sometimes outlandish) plan, the Lord shows Himself strong through our weakness, giving us reason to hope and the strength to persevere through perceived failure and humiliation.

When the Lord instructed Joshua to march around the walled city of Jericho for seven days, blow the ram horns and shout, Joshua knew this was not a viable military strategy if victory was the goal. But he chose to do it anyway.

When Elijah told Naaman to bathe seven times in the Jordan River to rid himself of leprosy, Naaman bristled at the suggestion, hoping for a less humiliating option. But Naaman decided to go to the Jordan anyway.

Even Jesus, at Lazarus's tomb, had the audacity to say, "Take away the stone."[32] Nothing about that act was going to be pretty, including the stench. His disciples, though still doubting a comeback, rolled back the stone anyway.

One of my favorite stories is that of David and Goliath. A simple shepherd boy and youngest of Jesse's eight sons, David faced his brothers' ridicule when he met Saul's army in the Elah Valley where they greeted him with, "Why have you come down? And with whom have you left those few sheep in the wilderness?"[33] You know there had to be more to their relationship than what the Text revealed when David replied, "What have I done now?"

David and Goliath is a classic narrative of expected failure. Everything about the story appeared impossible. King Saul, fearful himself to don the armor and fight the massive Goliath, doubted the boy David would succeed. But the underdog David held a vision in His heart—a faith built over years of shepherding. And he was counting on God's miraculous intervention. As he fingered the five stones in his pocket, David didn't weigh the odds and take a survey before facing the Philistine from Gath. He just ran toward the giant with faith and a plan, and an anticipated disaster became an incredible victory. He *dared* to imagine the unseen and became part of the improbable.

I'll let you in on a secret. When I watch any type of competition, I root for the underdog: whoever happens to be behind. Over the course of the event, the lead may change, and so does who I root for. I'm not a loyal fan. But I am passionate about a comeback! I have a thing for watching teams win that aren't supposed to, for an addict to turn their life around, for the woman from the projects to develop a thriving business, and for those who have faithfully walked through immeasurable loss to choose to help others do the same. The successful path of an underdog exhilarates me. Unfortunately, for an underdog to experience an amazing reversal, they must first *be* an underdog, which again presupposes the agony of weakness, loss, or frequent failure. Lazarus couldn't experience the miracle of being raised from the dead without first being dead. And I'm pretty sure no one would choose that path just to be part of a comeback.

The perceived limitations and endless ridicule we receive when we find ourselves in the position of an underdog will batter our faith, making it feel ludicrous to remain faithful. At times, the failings can be overwhelming. I would be naïve to think the only underdogs are athletes or competitors and that all comebacks are thrilling and joyous. The most powerful stories are not so glorious and involve intense battles. Those battles may include victimizing childhood abuse, struggling to maintain healthy relationships, fighting against familial destructive behavior, or trying to escape painful fallout memories of past experiences. Or they may include the debilitating shame of a poor decision, a contentious divorce, a regrettable affair, a financial misstep, jail time, an unexpected pregnancy, or harmful words uttered out of spite or anger.

Failure.

The heaviness of your story may have convinced you it is impossible to move forward or to ever forgive yourself; the trauma is too great and the transgression unredeemable. To add insult to injury, the enemy bombards you with thoughts that what has been done to you, or the choices that you made, disqualify you from receiving God's love, from serving Him, or from being able to love others well.

They are *all* lies. Yes, being an underdog is brutal, but it is *never* final.

The Most Spectacular Reversal

Our perception of the Lord and our expectation that He will do things as He has always done diminishes His greatness. Which is why we have difficulty believing the Bible. We arrogantly question God's existence and the vast love of Jesus that He could have died in our place to offer us relationship with God the Father. To *dare* believe such claims requires a brazen faith to leap across the chasm of doubt and step out into the unknown. Are we willing to blaze a new trail and trust Him when we don't understand? Ignoring His voice when it sounds irrational and when it throws us into the role of an underdog allows fear to win, and we miss out on what God really wants to do in and through us.

There were times I felt prompted to obey my parents, my coaches, my administrators, or to follow what I knew was right, and I shrugged it off. This time I wanted to be different. I wanted to trust what the Lord said to me about Mitch. Strengthened by the Spirit, I aspired to persevere like Abraham, who for twenty-five years embodied the life of an underdog and stayed the course, believing that even though all human reason for hope was gone, God would bring life to his impotent body and an improbable pregnancy to Sarah.[34]

That kind of remarkable faith to break through obstacles and step out to follow God—whether illustrated in the Text or through our own experiences—ignites a fire in my soul for the improbable. But the narrative I never tire of hearing, arguably the most misunderstood, miraculous, and unexpected of all time, is that of Jesus Christ. The Son of God who, in all His immenseness, humbled Himself to come as a baby born in a cave near Bethlehem. Raised by a young couple in the derided town of Nazareth, Jesus grew to live a sinless and holy life of love, mercy, and forgiveness, yet He was still criticized and hated. Just three years into His ministry, amid mocking and unbridled scorn, Jesus was betrayed, humiliated, beaten, crucified, and placed in a tomb, crushing all Messianic hopes.

But just outside the city wall of Jerusalem, the most spectacular underdog reversal of all time was in the making. In one majestic weekend Jesus broke all the rules. He rose from the dead, shattering the odds once and for all as He conquered sin, death, and the evil one. The Underdog who, in everyone's limited vision, had been finally and completely defeated, turned the tables and won!

What we choose to do with Jesus will change our lives forever. Will we *dare* to believe Jesus is who He says He is and that one day He will bring restoration to all things? Will we *dare* to place our lives in His hands, even when doing so doesn't make sense, even when the pain feels unjust, even when failure appears inescapable? Or will we ignore Jesus' boundless love and choose instead to trust in ourselves?

Though what I saw didn't make sense, I decided to trust Jesus with Mitch.

We can imagine the impossible, strategize for great accomplishments, and even assent to faith in some higher being. But not until we *dare* to faithfully submit our lives to the One who has paid the debt for our sin through His death and resurrection—choosing to live that out with all our heart, soul, mind, and strength—will we go from being an underdog to having the Spirit of the living God alive in us.[35] And through each painful and inevitable failure, the presence of the Lord will infuse us with a reason to hope and with the ability to persevere through it all.

Chapter 6

THE BEST SHAPE EVER

Irarely refuse an invitation to attend a women's basketball game. Often when I enter an arena in Michigan I run into former players or teammates, and this night was no exception. While laughing at the exaggerated stories of my coaching flaws, I glanced over their shoulders and was startled to see Mitch walk into the gym with his group of friends. My palms immediately started to sweat.

I wish I felt more confident.

After a pleasant wave of acknowledgment, I headed with my friends to the bleachers. They had no idea the words I held in my heart about Mitch. A few minutes later he entered the stands and took a seat two rows in front of us. We couldn't help but overhear him describe to his buddies the gift he bought his girlfriend for Christmas. My stomach churned. *I don't want to hear this. Why did he have to sit so close to me?*

Knowing Mitch was dating felt like a punch in the gut. As the conversation ensued about his girlfriend, my heart grew heavy. It hit a new low when she joined the group. My insecurities intensified as I struggled to stay out of the comparison trap. Words of doubt pounded against the sea wall of my heart like a category five hurricane: *You're not hearing from God. Waiting for Mitch is a waste of time. Your best years are passing by and you can't even date!*

This was not playing out how I imagined. The emotional surge ransacking my body reminded me of the pain and heartache of losing my coaching job. As I shared earlier, the pursuit of my coaching dreams ended with an abrupt firing. My anger toward administrators for invalidating their commitment seemed reasonable. No doubt my youthfulness exacerbated the feelings of injustice. The sudden thwarting of my plans and the resentment directed at those responsible caused considerable angst. But there is more to that coaching story…

Up until losing a very public job, my life had not held severe trauma, tragedy, or lasting wounds (and I thank God for that). But having what I loved ripped away shredded my heart. Being fired felt like the ultimate betrayal, no matter how I tried to spin it. Although the team's that I coached experienced unprecedented success, I still beat myself up for being unable to stop them from letting me go. The bottomless pit in my stomach made navigating the hurt feel unfair. As they watched me pack up my office and then took away my key, I vacillated between anger and despondency.

Some people purposefully inflict pain, leave carnage in their wake, and exhibit no emotional response. And others through simple ignorance (or their own woundedness) do the same. Firing me from my coaching job was not a deliberate attempt to harm me—*yet it did.* It made me want to yell at somebody. Truth be told, my flesh wished all the teams at that college would lose for the next ten years. Every team but mine, of course, which returned all but one player. I needed validation that my efforts made a difference.

In the tension God felt distant. Even my prayers seemed to ricochet off the ceiling. I collapsed alone on my living room floor. *Lord, all I have left is You!* I sobbed. I wanted God to be enough, but my spirit was crushed. Through the tears I sensed Jesus smile at my revelation as if He had been patiently waiting for this day. For years I believed the

Lord loved me, but right then I was hurled into trusting Him with that reality. In that irritating moment of ambivalence, I sensed His gentle Spirit urge me to reach out to those responsible for letting me go and confess my part in the bitterness that remained.

What?

You've got to be kidding!

Not a chance.

So much for obedience.

That prompting had to originate from the Lord because *nothing* in me thought that was a good idea. It made *no* sense at all! Why would I want to go back to the scene of the crime? I know following God is a choice, but I purposefully drove out of my way to avoid even passing by the gym. No way I wanted to enter the building. The thought of sitting in a room with the same people who stripped me of my passion was the *last* thing I wanted to do—especially since our previous encounter was anything but positive.

The Spirit continued to whisper to my heart and gently nudge me to go back until I knew I needed to *dare* step out and obey. Three weeks after being fired, I contacted the college administrators who let me go and asked for a meeting. They agreed. Trembling, I stepped into their office. Nothing in me wanted to be there. *Lord, give me the right words to say . . . and the ability to say them.* As I confessed my bitterness concerning their decision to let me go and asked their forgiveness for my anger, they stared at me in stunned silence.

Surprisingly enough, that meeting was the beginning of freedom.

Nothing changed in my situation as a result of my obedience. I was still out of a job. But a deep and inexplicable peace began to replace the bitterness. The Lord was reshaping me into something new in a way only He could. Within days, the Spirit encouraged me to take another step: to love my enemies and pray for those who persecuted me.[36] To pray for those who betrayed me, for the assistant coach who went after my position, and for the team to succeed without me.

It was agonizing.

My attempts at prayer were feeble at best. *Lord, give the new coach wisdom. Help the team adjust. Create unity among the players. May You be glorified in their pain . . . and may You somehow be glorified in mine.*

As days turned to weeks and eventually into months, my prayers lacked enthusiasm, yet I persisted. And every time I chose to follow the Lord—regardless of the fact my heart wasn't in it—He changed my thoughts, which in turn altered how I felt. Throughout my emotional makeover, I tried to speak positively about the program and to validate those words by my actions (somedays were markedly easier than others). Slowly, the disappointment and anger started to dissipate.

This heartfelt transformation into God's best shape ever required a better understanding of forgiveness, an openness to continually receive it, and a willingness to graciously offer it to another no matter how I felt. Which for me now meant I needed to start to pray for Mitch, and his girlfriend.

Shaped for His Use

When the Lord works to shape me, it is often uncomfortable and accomplished in ways I never anticipated. I remember taking a pottery class and liking it so much I bought a miniature potter's wheel. I spent hours forming treasured masterpieces. But before I could create, I had to add water and pound the cold, gray mass to make it pliable. Repeatedly, I pressed and folded the clay until I had eliminated all the air bubbles. Once I'd completed the preparation, the clay was ready to be transformed on the wheel.

When I succumbed to my impatience and skipped the preparation step, the clay ended up too difficult to work with and I had to start over.

We're like that too. We prefer an instantaneous molding of our life into a piece of outstanding artistry, which tempts us to avoid the painstaking process of preparation. Preparation is grueling. Whether you are a musician, student, businessperson, or first-time parent, you will experience seasons reminiscent of the movie *Groundhog Day*, where each day is a repeat of the one before. The recurring monotony threatens to slow our progress and fade our dreams into the horizon. To make matters worse, when you finally make it off the table and onto the proverbial wheel to be shaped into a gorgeous work of art, your efforts produce another air pocket of failure, and you return to be pressed again.

While the preparation is wearisome, the shaping isn't much better. More than once, the frustration of spinning like clay on a wheel—painfully repeating the same lesson again and again—made me want to bail and jump off. *There must be a better option. I'm feeling nauseated.* (Plus, I never liked merry-go-rounds.) Impatience was effectively driving my desire to do something besides twirl on God's wheel in a "molding" pattern.

Heeding the Lord's voice requires effort, and repetition and preparation are a necessary part of His plan. Some situations arise in which we need to act, to "trust in the Lord, and do good."[37] However, Jesus would rather work *in* us than *through* us, and our *being* in relationship with Him is way more important than our working *for* Him. For in His presence on His wheel—when life is hard, and friends are distant—His faithful love proves to be enough as He molds us more and more into His likeness.

Several days I wake up confident that perfection is just one spin away, then God launches work in another area of my life and around I go again. This is no truer than in the realm of forgiveness. Nothing cripples me more than refusing to forgive. It suppresses the ability of my spirit to hear from the Lord and takes a toll on my mental and physical health. Even worse, it strains my relationship with God and with others.

Repeatedly the Lord has kept me on His wheel to fashion in me a habit of forgiveness. Although the path to freedom that grants mercy to us and to others is simple, it's rarely easy, and it's nearly impossible to carry out on our own. The only way I could truly forgive myself was to rely on the Holy Spirit as my power source. And the only way I could forgive those who hurt me (maliciously or not) and pray for them was to tap into His available strength. To allow Him to comfort me in my grief and enable me to forgive. To realize that it is His joy that strengthens my heart.[38]

Over and over, I found myself needing to blindly trust that the Lord would give me the ability to do the right thing (like humbly asking for forgiveness and graciously giving it away), because nothing in me felt like being obedient. And He did. But to be transformed into God's best shape ever, I first needed to gain a greater understanding of how I had been forgiven.

Receive Jesus' Forgiveness First

God has always desired relationship with us but the sin that occurred in the garden of Eden and that now lives in our hearts would forever separate us from Him without some sort of perfect restitution. As part of God's master plan, He sent His Son, Jesus, to pay our debt with His life. When we say yes to Jesus as our Lord and Savior, He grants us a miraculous forgiveness of sins. Past. Present. Future. Humbly acknowledging that Jesus' death on the cross paid the penalty for the way we have missed the mark and partnered with the enemy, opens the door for the Holy Spirit to begin the process of sculpting our cold clay heart into His best shape ever.

To truly forgive ourselves and those who hurt us, we must first recognize the depth of our own depravity and receive the forgiveness Jesus offers. We remain unable to extend forgiveness or fear asking others for it when we can't imagine ever being forgiven. Our own regrets hinder us from embracing the mercy of Christ and we instead come into agreement with the lies of the evil one: *No one cares about you. You deserve what happened. God will never forgive you for what you've done.* Believing these lies keeps us from experiencing genuine freedom.

(On a side note, it is easy to become confused as to whether the thoughts you hear in your head are from you, the enemy, other people, or from God. This may help: when what you hear uses the word *I* instead of *you*, it's probably your thought. It's probably originating from you. For instance, *I am frustrated,* or *I am going to be late,* are your honest thoughts. And *You are loved with an everlasting love* or *You're doing well,* are just the kind of encouraging words you would hear from the Holy Spirit. However, *You will never amount to anything* or *You are unworthy of being loved,* are lies the enemy or other people have thrown at you. We need to get really good at identifying and rejecting the lies.)

Forgiveness is a powerful and priceless gift to us from God that once received it can in turn be given away. Accepting His tender love massages the hardened recesses of our wounded hearts, and, like clay, we begin to soften in the Potter's hands. With the softening, He then sculpts us through our life experiences to become more compassionate, sensitive, and gracious. Those who recognize and accept God's extravagant forgiveness—forgiveness that chases us down even when we betray Him—are empowered to offer the same to someone else. To gift what we've been given. By choosing to walk through the process of forgiveness, we break the control we gave others over us—control that creates fear, bitterness, anger, and resentment—and we take back the space we allowed them to occupy in our minds.

But we don't have to forgive. We don't have to move toward recovery and reconciliation. The choice is ours. When hurt or offended (purposefully or not) by an employer or even a potential boyfriend, my natural recourse is to get even. Payback seems much more logical to me. Nicole Kidman, playing Sylvia Broome in the movie *The Interpreter*, offered this perspective:

> "Everyone who loses somebody wants revenge on someone, on God if they can't find anyone else. But in Africa, in Matobo, the Ku believe that the only way to end grief is to save a life.
>
> If someone is murdered, a year of mourning ends with a ritual that we call the drowning man trial. There's an all-night party beside the river. At dawn, the killer is put in a boat. He's taken out on the water and he's dropped. He's bound so that he can't swim.
>
> The family of the dead then has to make a choice. They can let him drown or they can swim out and save him. The Ku believe that if the family lets the killer drown, they'll have justice but spend the rest of their lives in mourning. But if they save him—if they admit that life isn't always just—that very act can take away their sorrow. Vengeance is a lazy form of grief."[39]

Sometimes I just want to be lazy. I want to hurt those who have hurt me. The problem is, it's not biblical and will only make matters worse. We probably know that. Holy Spirit-inspired forgiveness doesn't leave room for revenge. Unfortunately, many harmful and destructive opinions on how a believer *should* forgive exist and they often come from the church. *Forgive and forget; don't tell anyone; they didn't mean it; pretend it didn't happen; Christians are meant to unjustly suffer.*

While we can find glimmers of truth in each of those statements, they remain distorted. And this warped view of forgiveness has permeated and damaged our culture. As Tim Mackie, founder of The Bible Project suggests, "Forgiveness is not ignoring or forgetting, it is not condoning or excusing, it is not tolerating or allowing further abuse, it is not reconciliation or restoration, it is not returning back to the way things were before, and it is not allowing offenders to escape consequences."[40]

When we forgive it doesn't mean the other person is right and the offender is granted license to hurt us again. And it doesn't imply legal ramifications are unjustified or that boundaries shouldn't be put in place. Granting forgiveness does not restore trust, but it might start the recovery process. We may choose to forgive because the Lord tells us to or because we desire freedom from bondage, and He offers it. Whatever the reason, forgiveness makes the decision to no longer let the offender continue to inflict pain in us by holding on to the offense. Forgiveness gives up our right to get even. Forgiveness reaches out in love.

We all know individuals or people groups who will never receive justice for what happened to them or to their family members. No amount of money or jail time will ever make up for what they lost. James, the half-brother of Jesus, wrote, "Mercy triumphs over judgment."[41] Which could be taken to mean, mercy triumphs over justice. But mercy—or better said, Christ-centered *love*—trumps justice. The loving act of forgiveness is more powerful than justice to restore what has been broken. In fact, love may very well *be* justice.

But instead of love, we cling to the destructiveness of anger, bitterness, blame, and shame, which in turn halts our spiritual growth, hardens our hearts, and damages our bodies. It keeps us out of fellowship with the Lord and hinders us from fulfilling the call of God on our lives in this generation. When we refuse to forgive as Jesus teaches and choose instead to slander our neighbor and remain hostile to the one who hurt us, even our prayers are repulsive to God.[42] But when we extend or receive forgiveness, lives heal in ways that cannot be reasoned out. It is supernatural. And it centers on love. It centers on Jesus.

Send It Away

Stepping out in a single moment to ask forgiveness of those who fired me may have been obedient, but my mind still battled a rise of negative thoughts, making the daily choice to forgive the hurt a necessity. Forgiveness, while an uncomfortable process, possesses power. As I wrestled with this abstract idea of forgiveness, within hours of each other, two different pastors shared with me that Jesus taught His disciples to forgive using the Greek word *aphiēmi*, an action verb meaning to leave behind or send away.[43] (The unique timing alone told me the Lord was making a point I needed to hear.) By creating a word picture, Jesus helped the disciples see that forgiveness required them to do something. That to completely forgive we need to leave the offense behind or send it away. I used to think it was enough simply to say, "I forgive you," then do my best not to feel resentful. My perception of what was necessary to repeatedly forgive included limited action on my part. I had no idea I could do more.

Sending away the pain of betrayal or leaving behind the trauma of abuse begins a process to change everything. But *where* do we send the wounds of infidelity or leave the tragedy of deceit? How do we release ourselves from the regrets riddling our lives and deal with the aftermath?

We send away the sins of others—the lies, words, and actions done against us or our loved ones—the same place we leave behind our own. At the feet of Jesus. At the foot of His cross. It makes sense. It's the place where the most redemptive and wondrous work was ever done.

> The cross is where He paid for our sins.
> The cross is where we abandon the sins of others.
> The cross is where the forgiving love of Jesus fashions us into the best shape ever.
> The cross is where Jesus offers the power to restore our soul.
> The cross is where miracles happen.

Freedom from holding onto an offense (which literally holds on to us) is available when we choose to release our grip and leave the offense at the cross. This can be done by making a specific list of those who hurt or disappointed us, then one at a time, pray out loud to let go of every insult, attack, or injustice by sending each one and its associated pain to Jesus. When we make the daily choice to send our sins and those of others to Jesus, He breaks strongholds that deter us from becoming beautifully shaped for His use. This simple action allows our hearts to experience a newly found freedom. And when we choose to walk in that freedom, the Holy Spirit empowers us to love well. Our relationships experience amazing healing when we send our offenses to the cross.

Unpleasant memories or feelings you have buried for years might be breaking through to the surface, and you just can't imagine letting go or forgiving those who were responsible for such immense loss or unimaginable pain. Will you *dare* to send their offense to the cross? Will you *dare* to let Jesus begin to heal your heart and lead you to freedom?

I am not thrilled that God keeps providing me with opportunities to forgive (reshaping me like a lump of clay) until He reminds me how often I inflict pain and need forgiveness. When I speak harsh words or hold onto unresolved anger, the Lord offers me such incredible love and grace I can then release others from their own failures.

Sending away a real or perceived offense indicates an awareness of how I have been forgiven and a willingness to forgive myself. Praying for those who offend me has become an everyday part of my shaping process. Prayer provides supernatural power that develops an intimacy with the One we pray to, the one we pray with, and the one we pray for. Prayer continues to turn our hearts to Jesus again and again as He shapes us on His wheel.

Agreeing to forgive also involves a conscious choice to speak good about those who hurt us, to support them in their pursuits, and to congratulate them in their successes. Ouch. This is as counterintuitive as it gets. I knew the Lord wanted me to be gracious to Mitch's girlfriend, but rarely do I feel like encouraging those who cause me pain. Only by *daring* to walk this out (despite feelings to the contrary) was I then able to experience the power and presence of the Lord and obtain a greater knowledge of His grace. Celebrating those who hurt us, through our words or our actions, destroys the ability the evil one has in controlling that area of our lives.

A significant part of my journey toward freedom from the debilitating power of resentment happened nearly a year after being fired from my college coaching job. While I sat in the bleachers watching the team I poured my life into for six years win a national championship without me, the Lord worked in my heart. As officials prepared the award presentation following a spectacular come-from-behind win, the Spirit stirred me to step out and make my way around the court. Unnoticed by fans and players, I approached the coach who took over my job less than a year before, shook her hand, and congratulated her on a remarkable win.

Freedom.

I would be lying if I said twinges of pain from that experience never come back, but they are faint, and I know forgiveness has been granted. It helped me then and even now to purposefully support the coach and the college even when it hurts.

Nearly a decade later, I crossed paths with the same coach who played a significant role in removing me from my position. The Holy Spirit had been refashioning her heart over the years as well, and in a surprising exchange, she apologized for the decisions she made that led to my firing and asked for my forgiveness. And in that moment, I again offered what Jesus gave me. Forgiveness.

I soon returned to coach softball at a nearby university and basketball at the local high school. In that first season back, my coaching decisions came under fire by two irate parents. (These situations are inescapable … we need to understand forgiveness!) Their toxic comments to fans and players led to a meeting with me, the athletic director, and both parents. For an hour and a half, they chose to direct their anger at my character. I leaned heavily on the Lord to endure unwarranted criticism with little response. The Spirit urged me not to defend myself but rather listen to their concerns and highlight their daughter's ability, work ethic, and integrity. Prior to the meeting I jotted down verses on my notepad to keep me from losing my focus (and my temper), and throughout our conversation, Isaiah 53:7 became my prayer: "He was oppressed, and he was afflicted, yet he opened not his mouth; like a lamb that is led to the slaughter, and like a sheep that before its shearers is silent, so he opened not his mouth." By the end of our meeting, the parents (both lawyers) walked away encouraged and somewhat confused by the disparity between their viewpoint and reality.

It is unnatural for me to be the first to apologize or to stay silent when cornered. I would rather respond with a deluge of justifications to defend my actions. And during that encounter I had good ones. But the Holy Spirit (who I believe found a permanent place for me on this wheel) kept saying: *Choose to forgive and leave the offense at the cross. They are not your responsibility, they are Mine.* His words revolved in my mind like a song on repeat.

Although I didn't feel like it, I pictured myself laying their accusations right where Jesus paid the price for me. The cross. Now when people intentionally or unintentionally wound me or even step out of relationship with me, I consciously place my desires, identity, and heartache at the foot of His cross and trust the Lord to do something in my heart and in theirs that I can't yet see. I no longer want to keep people on my hook (as though my assignment is to fix them), I want them on His. It's not about changing anyone else but me.

We must be careful when talking about forgiveness, reconciliation, and restoration. In many circumstances, forgiveness is necessary but reestablishing the relationship is neither possible nor recommended. Offering forgiveness does not automatically restore trust, neither does it imply that trust should be restored. When we find ourselves in a destructive situation, we need to seek out assistance for our own safety and that of others.[44]

By *daring* in faith to do the hard thing, we allow the Lord to continue to shape us on His wheel. And as He does, our confidence grows in His desire to complete the work He started, even if it happens on the day we see Him face to face. Until that glorious moment, I want to remain pliable and willing to fight for freedom.

The evil one will never be able to withstand the truth of God's love as we wield the weapon of forgiveness from our arsenal. For through forgiveness, the work of the cross becomes a part of us. When we accept

His forgiveness, when we forgive ourselves, and when we forgive others, our hearts open to the Lord and His love pours in. And the flowing love of His Spirit will allow us to *dare* follow in faith as He transforms us into the best shape ever: "For freedom Christ has set us free; stand firm therefore, and do not submit again to a yoke of slavery."[45]

True freedom. There is nothing like it.

Forgiveness Prayer

A sample prayer, like the one below, has helped me be intentional in pursuing the healing power of forgiveness in my heart and in my relationships. Even if the feelings aren't there at the time, saying the words out loud—even daily—will allow a supernatural transformation to begin.

Heavenly Father, thank You for the incredible power of forgiveness available because of Jesus. Right now, I accept Your forgiveness for the many ways I have failed You, and I forgive myself too. I also choose to forgive those individuals who have hurt me. Many times, I have not loved but instead have resented people who have wounded, offended, or disappointed me. I have held unforgiveness in my heart toward them. I call upon You, Lord, to help me to forgive. I do now choose to forgive [name them, both living and dead]. I ask You, Lord, to pour out Your love on each one of them. Rework my heart to love them well too.

Transform my thoughts and allow me to see how marvelously You made me. I place my offenses, my expectations, my relationships, my hopes, and my dreams at the foot of Your cross. Help me walk in righteousness, peace, and joy, demonstrating Your life here on earth. Help me to assume the best as I choose to be kind and compassionate, quickly forgiving others just as You forgave me. Thank You for the promise of forgiveness and for Your amazing love. Amen.

Chapter 7

TOGETHER IN THE VALLEY

The morning sun glistened off the freshly fallen snow as I drove downtown. Singing on a praise team fills my soul yet having a Sunday morning off felt refreshing. The open weekend created a wonderful opportunity to visit a new church pastored by a friend and his wife. I found an empty seat in the middle of the chapel, excited for worship. As music filled the room, I was surprised to see Mitch coming down the side aisle. When he entered my row, girlfriend in hand, my stomach lurched. He grabbed the seat next to mine, and with a wink and a smile, he squeezed my hand. I said hello and after politely leaning forward to greet his girlfriend, I quickly turned to face the front. My excitement now quashed.

Mitch had spoken highly of this fellowship of believers before, but he regularly attended elsewhere. I had no idea he would show up that day. To make matters worse, Mitch looked great, but I could barely stomach seeing his arm around someone else.

The service became a blur. I prayed through most of it. *Lord, this is unbearable. Couldn't You have guided Mitch and his girlfriend to some other seat or some other church?*

When the service ended, I made a dash for the nearest exit. A gracious gentleman greeted me while I tried to leave, and I was barely cordial. I wanted out of there.

I sobbed the whole way home. *This is so hard! It's been five years now. Lord, am I still where You want me to be?*

Holding on to the vision that I was to marry Mitch kept stripping away my layers of pride, self-sufficiency, and independence. I knew the choice fell on me to follow the call or walk away, to stop the pain or *dare* keep risking failure. But I also knew the Holy Spirit had purposely led me to what Oswald Chambers called the valley, "to batter us into the shape of the vision."[46] I just thought I should have made it through by now.

A valley is that low area of land between mountain peaks or foothills, which at night is especially challenging to find your way out of. And traversing a valley in life feels much the same. It is a struggle. Successful passage requires more than just endurance. If you have ever hiked in a wilderness, you know valleys are commonplace and seem to emerge out of nowhere.

My mind and emotions were engaged in a battle over the wisdom of my choice to go with the Lord into a place so dark and unpredictable.

The ten-minute drive home after church felt like forever. I burst through the front door and ran inside. As I slumped into a heap on my bed, tears began soaking the pillow. Encountering Mitch so unexpectedly that morning revealed the waves of insecurity still present in my heart.

Lord, I need help!

After a lengthy dose of self-pity, the phone rang, and I hurriedly tried to pull myself together. On the other end was a godly woman aware I held a vision in my heart about marriage but not privy to the details. She had been at church that morning too, but we never connected. While I nursed the sting of continual failure and rejection, she asked abruptly, "Has God told you that you are to marry Mitch Carver?"

My heart skipped a beat. "Why would you say that?" I asked guardedly. "Did you see him sit next to me at church this morning?"

"No. I didn't see Mitch at all. And the first time I saw you, you were walking to the parking lot after the service. God simply put both of you on my heart today."

Her confirmation that afternoon was a flicker of light in a dark valley. It infused me with the courage to hold on, even in the middle of stifling disappointment.

Sometimes we choose to stay in a difficult situation because we know it may ultimately produce (either in us or in our relationships) what the Lord desires and what we may one day desire too. It's what compels us to work long shifts as a nurse, get up early to go to the gym, push ourselves to reach the quota, or work two jobs to provide for our family. This isn't a valley we stumble into or is forced upon us. We *dare* to enter this valley on our own volition.

Despite the heartache and the temptation to say no before God did, I stepped deeper into the valley. I chose to believe the Lord would walk with me; that He would hold my hand and guide me; that with His presence would come His power. I chose to believe I wouldn't be alone. For me, this faith journey was no longer about *how* to walk a road less traveled, but rather *with whom*. Partnering in community, even when our only community is Jesus, is formidable. And at that moment, I needed Him to sustain my spirit.

For years I had dismissed the prayer "Jesus be with me" as trite. He was already supposed to be everywhere, I shouldn't have to pray for it. But deciding to travel through a valley where I had to cling to Jesus—where His strength held me up and His voice soothed my soul—altered this reality. "Jesus be with me" meant we were teammates. He wasn't a spectator watching from afar, He became personally involved. I chose to believe the power of His presence would lead me through uncertain days and keep me from walking away. And should the unexpected threaten to overtake me (like a Mitch encounter at church), the Lord's presence in the valley would enable me to persevere and stay the course. The decision to rely on Him to be enough, alters every storm-ridden valley for anyone who follows.

We find a great example of this in the fourth chapter of Mark's Gospel. Large crowds had gathered near the Sea of Galilee to hear Jesus, who for hours engaged them and spoke with unparalleled authority. By the time evening came, Jesus said to His disciples, "Let us go across to the other side."[47] So the disciples hopped in a boat with Jesus and headed out. Before long, a storm arose. Waves smashed against the side of the small craft, beginning to fill it with water. And yet, exhausted from a full day's activities, Jesus slept soundly at the stern. Thrown into disarray, the disciples frantically awakened Him. He calmed the wind and the waves, then told His disciples, "Why are you so afraid? Have you still no faith?"[48]

The Text provides a baffling glimpse into what following the Lord looks like. The disciples, while sailing across the sea (as Jesus directed), ended up in the middle of a storm. Right where He wanted them to be. But the way Jesus responded to their fear makes me wonder if they should have let Him sleep or at least not rouse Him in such a panic. In their defense, if I were in a boat taking on water, I would shove a bucket into everyone's hands, including the guy sleeping in the back. It's not my style to wait out a storm fearfully clasping an oar.

But maybe Jesus wanted the disciples to exhibit a more *daring* faith. Maybe He wanted them to calm the sea; to speak to the storm; to simply trust that He led them there and that the power of His presence in the boat would be enough. *Daring* faith asks us to look at the situation from a vantage point other than that of the valley. It requires that we see God as intricately involved and immensely powerful right where we are.

However, in those trying moments when we have been steered into our own tumultuous valley, what does it look like *when faith dares?*

I believe it is way more than my comfort allows.

At a young age I committed my life to Christ, was baptized and raised by believing parents, and I felt comfortable following those who chased after Jesus. Namely my mom and dad. I held onto their faith as if it were mine. Now I needed to chase after Jesus myself. I needed to own my journey and live out what I said I believed about God, no matter how difficult. Sadly, a valley is an annoying aberration to our perceived vision of how our days should unfold. And when the valley blindsides us, our normal feels unfairly stripped away. We need *daring* faith that our relationship with the Lord (not the relationship our parents, grandparents, friends, or pastor might have with Him) will comfort our spirit, infuse us with hope, and deliver what we need right when we need it.

Valleys create a frightening and inescapable reality. At any given time, we may very well be approaching a valley, fighting our way through one, or on our way out. By choosing to follow the Lord into a valley (or to the other side of the sea), we can be assured He is there with us too. As the psalmist David reminds us, "Even though I walk through the valley of the shadow of death, I will fear no evil, for you are with me; your rod and your staff, they comfort me."[49] His rod of protection and guiding staff provide overwhelming comfort when we take our eyes off the storm and focus on Jesus. His presence makes it possible to maintain solid footing in a valley. It just doesn't take away our struggle.

Struggle for the Vision

Don't get me wrong, I'm all for making life easier. I'm thrilled I never had to do laundry with a washboard or learn how to use the slide rule. But hard is good for us too. There is something about working all summer long to earn money to buy a bicycle that makes us appreciate the ride.

Unfortunately, our culture would rather avoid hard. Young people get rewarded for showing up and parents give in to the temptation to prevent children from owning the consequences of their actions. Even adults can't escape the draw of tranquility. We love having the world at our fingertips and can become miffed when mending a relationship or finding a new job requires effort. But I believe we can do hard. We can struggle through a valley with Jesus and come out better on the other side. Gravitating toward the easy path, however, is *really* tempting.

In the book of Genesis, we don't find much written about Abram's father, Terah, other than he left Ur for Canaan with his family but never made it. He settled in Haran and died there.[50] The next thing we read is God telling Abram to "go from your country and your kindred and your father's house to the land that I will show you."[51] Maybe Abram's father, Terah, received the same call from the Lord as his son, we don't know. We do know Terah stopped when the goal was Canaan. He gave up on the vision once it became a struggle.

When a valley is imminent, I become anxious about how it will rock my world. If I were Abram and the Lord told me to leave my family but didn't mention the destination or the ensuing journey, I don't know if I would have followed. And if I were his wife, Sarai, I surely would have unleashed a myriad of questions before I left for nowhere. It's hard enough to stick with God's plan when I *know* where He wants me to go.

Coming face to face with a long, rocky, and unfamiliar trail through a valley makes the thought of moving forward daunting. It is much easier to settle. To be honest, entering a place where I know I will be stretched, battered, or pounded on like a lump of clay doesn't cause me to jump for joy. My maturity has not yet grown to a point where I embody what James described when he wrote, "Count it all joy, my brothers, when you meet trials of various kinds."[52] When trials come my way, joy is definitely not my default. I crave the path of least resistance, not one requiring I abandon the security of the known, let alone my comfort.

But Abram, on his journey from Haran, didn't wander around a desert with the hope of eventually finding his way to some random place. The Lord led Abram right where He wanted him to go. They traveled together. God wants to lead us too, because He knows intimacy grows in the valley and He is all about relationship. Even when the Lord instructed Moses and the people of Israel to make Him a sanctuary in the barren land near Mt. Horeb, it wasn't about finding a residence. Rather, He said, "Make me a sanctuary, that I may dwell *in their midst.*"[53]

The Lord wanted to be *with* His people then and He wants our lives to be intertwined with His now. He wants to laugh with us and share in our tears. He wants us to vent our troubles to Him so He can prove Himself faithful. Allowing the Lord to connect *with* us—as we talk with Him, listen for His voice, and allow Him to lead—increases our trust that He is who He says He is. And it is there in our valley, when we can't see what lies ahead and the struggle feels relentless, that the power of His presence and the truth of His Word will embolden our weak faith and inspire us to *dare* dream again.

At the ford of the Jabbok River, Jacob (Abram's grandson) feared reuniting with his brother, Esau, who had threatened to kill him.[54] He sent his family on ahead with gifts of appeasement, then using a rock for a pillow, tried to sleep. Knowing you were about to meet someone who wanted you dead might produce a restless night or two. But Jacob didn't just toss and turn, he physically wrestled with Jesus, the Angel of the Lord. All night long they grappled, and Jacob refused to let go until he was blessed. Along with a blessing he received a new name: *Israel.* Meaning to struggle with or to contend with God.[55] Jacob, now Israel, struggled with the Lord that night and was blessed. He struggled *with* the Lord; he didn't struggle *against* Him. Before the name change, Jacob (whose name means supplanter: a person who usurps the position of another) already struggled *against* people. And he grappled, wrestled, and struggled with being who God wanted him to be. We do it too. Whether our struggle is with finances, relationships, or even our vision, the Lord desires to struggle *with* us through it. When life is hard, He wants us to lean on Him for comfort, not fight against Him.

But time in the valley has the potential to shut down our ability to imagine and to dream. Our eyes see the all-encompassing darkness and we become disheartened. The Hebrew people continued to wander, seemingly aimlessly through the desert, when a young guy named Joshua witnessed unprecedented signs leading to their freedom. After thousands crossed the parted sea in a miraculous act of God, he left with his buddy Caleb and ten other guys to check out the promised land. Of the twelve, only he and Caleb returned with *daring* faith and a vision that the almighty God, who had brought His people out of bondage, would go before them to conquer the land. The other ten princes had lived in darkness so long that when they saw giants living in the land; they became blinded to the God possibilities. Sadly, the majority ruled, and instead of leading them to victory, God went with them into another valley. Their journey was not supposed to look like this. What should have been a celebration, turned instead, into a valley of death.

The problem we have is the reality of our valley experience seems to counter our vision making us question whether our fight is *with* God or *against* Him. We wonder why bad things happen to good people and doubt God is even paying attention. While opting to wrestle through our valley *with* God may not bring us out any faster, it will change our perspective, which in turn will alter the way we feel. And once our mind and emotions start to transform, so will our words and actions. We will no longer view our circumstances as fighting *against* the Lord for what we want, but as an opportunity to journey together *with* Him through a valley we cannot come through well on our own.

Journeying *with* Jesus was changing my heart.

We Need Community

I am not implying we are somehow meant to go it alone with the Lord. Quite the opposite. He designed people for connection; to travel with us through our valley, much like Jesus and His friends, Peter, James, and John. Because we are created in the image of God, we each embody a reflection of Him that, although incomplete, is unique. Our experience of who God is expands through consistent relationship with other image bearers. Authentic and honest connection with those who faithfully pray for me and those who have a deeper understanding of the Text than I do grows in me a profound measure of patience, gratefulness, and love. When the road is hard and feels never-ending, Jesus-centered community affords me the confidence to hope in the Lord just when I want to call it quits.

Living alone a good part of my life forced me to depend on others. (I had no idea you had to blow out sprinklers before winter or that furnace filters need to be changed more than once every five years. Thank God for wonderful neighbors!) Often when I encountered an unpleasant task at home or needed knowledge beyond my limited gift mix, I eagerly invited others to join me. (Did you know a basketball team can paint the outside of an entire house in a single day?)

Collaborating with friends to trim the bushes, stain the deck, or clean out the garage made projects feel effortless. Not because the workload was lighter (although it was), but because relationship brings joy when laboring together toward a shared purpose. It's why I am an ardent fan of team sports. Uniting with those willing to go down to the valley to be painfully battered into the shape of the vision to defeat a common adversary is energizing! Dreaded experiences (such as two-a-day practices or fitness-training sessions) become much more palatable and produce better outcomes when traversed in community. By choosing to tackle the grind together, what we deem impossible may very well be attainable.

For years, the United States experienced great success on the track-and-field world stage. Then in 1981, sponsors entered the picture. Instead of paying for second-tier runners to train with the elite, sponsors chose only to invest in the best. Without accessible, elite role models, college and high school runners ran slower. In the 1990s only nine male high school runners broke nine minutes for two miles, down from fifty-one runners in the 1980s and eighty-four in the 1970s. As fewer mid-level runners remained in the national program, the United States soon lost its dominance and had a dismal showing in the 2000 Olympic games, finishing no higher than sixth place in races longer than four hundred meters.

Trainers and coaches hypothesized that the loss of the *group effect* experienced in mixed running groups caused the demise. Post-collegiate running groups formed again with immediate results. American runners witnessed success over the next decade. And the trend continues. In 2014, twenty American high school boys ran two miles in less than nine minutes *in one meet*.[56]

We all need community—I would even go so far as to say we long for it. We were created for connection, to invigorate and bolster each other to pursue God's call. But for me, to understand the power of community and to trust others with my weaknesses and successes took time. It was a process to learn to lean on others to better fulfill the Lord's plan for my life. I much preferred to figure things out on my own. Which is why I love the story in Exodus 17, where the Israelites fought Amalek (king of the Amalekites) in the valley of Rephidim. The Israelites would prevail only if Moses stood on a hill overlooking the battle and held the staff above his head. Whenever Moses' arms grew heavy and he lowered the staff, Amalek dominated the fight. As the battle persisted, Moses grew tired. His brother, Aaron, and close friend Hur, who had climbed the mountain with Moses, recognized his inability to keep the staff in the air. So to save their fellow Israelites warring below, they sat Moses on a large rock and each grabbed an arm. They didn't take turns raising the staff themselves; Aaron and Hur simply supplied the strength to Moses' arms so he could do it. Exodus 17:12 says, "So his [Moses'] hands were *steady* until the going down of the sun."

And it worked! It counted! I'm not shocked the Lord defeated Amalek, He could have done that whether Moses held up the staff or not. I'm amazed that someone else holding up his arms counted as though he were doing it himself. Even though Moses needed the help of his friends to keep the staff over his head, the Lord still supplied the victory. The Text goes on to say Joshua and the men of Israel "overwhelmed Amalek and his people with the sword."[57] It didn't matter that Moses was incapable of holding the staff up on his own. In God's reality, it is totally acceptable (and maybe preferred) to rely on others to accomplish His call on our lives. Just as Moses needed Aaron and Hur to fulfill the Lord's purpose for Israel, the right community will enable us to do what we could never handle on our own too.

You may find it interesting that the word *steady*, from Exodus 17:12 above, in Hebrew is the word *emuwnah*. This same word can be translated as faithfulness or faith.[58] In other words, faithfulness (or faith) is best exemplified in community. I love that! Receiving faithful support from God's people—and returning the same—is an intricate component of following the Lord well in the valley.

What does your community look like? Who helps sustain you on the road to your vision? Even now a storm may be looming on your horizon that looks like a relocation, a court hearing, or a medical diagnosis, and you are desperate for a prop. While loyal and treasured friends may not possess the same call on their lives, the right ones are those willing to join you in the valley and hold up your arms as you pursue yours. It could be that your community consists of a close family member or a friend who sticks closer than a brother.[59] Yes, you may need to seek out your community, but you don't need to recruit hundreds off your Facebook page. A few quality people will do. You might even be surprised to discover your Bible study small group (the ones you were sure you shared nothing in common with) will step in wonderfully as your Aaron and Hur.

Even with the support of Moses' friends, the Israelites' defeat of Amalek in the valley of Rephidim so soon after leaving Egypt was remarkable. They had to push aside their fear and trust God (and their leaders) to keep from losing the battle. The Lord may lead us through a monumental victory but succumbing to the temptation of fear can suddenly drive us to change course.

On Mt. Carmel, for instance, Elijah had just called down fire from heaven to consume a sacrifice on an altar drenched in water, and God supernaturally showed up. Yet an astounding victory was not enough. After killing 450 prophets of Baal, Elijah feared for his life and ran more than one hundred miles to Beersheba, eventually ending up at the Sinai Mountain range (more than three hundred miles away). Shortly after, he petitioned God to take his life. After a true mountaintop experience, Elijah became fearful, exhausted, and despondent, sure everyone in Israel had forsaken God's covenant. But he was believing a lie. God preserved a remnant.[60] In Elijah's despair, the Lord was already preparing the way before him with a community who would help hold up his arms.

When the Lord gives us a vision that is not yet real, we must decide if we will follow Him into a valley on the way. But following requires obedience. Whether we sense the Lord guiding us through His living Word, through others, or through His Spirit, the choice remains: will we *dare* obey what we hear? The Lord may not ask us to call fire down upon an altar, but He may *dare* us to enter a valley to believe for a physical healing or the turnaround of a troubled child. In the struggle, we need to *dare* trust His heart even if it means we need to speak to our storm; betting our lives that Jesus will provide unexpected strength for every valley He takes us into.

Who Is God to You in the Valley?

During the Olympic games in Barcelona, Spain, I joined a sport-based ministry team to provide chapel services for competing athletes and coaches. In between daily chapels, we played basketball in universities and men's maximum-security prisons. Using the draw of sport in an electrified athletic environment enabled us to creatively share the gospel. One of our basketball players was a six-foot-nine-inch Harlem Globetrotter. Our success (even with a woman point guard) was assured because we were playing with André. Everyone knew he would dominate. All I had to do was get him the ball.

Do we view the Lord that way? How big is He to us when all we can see is the storm?

Since 2007, I have partnered with Under the Fig Tree Ministries[61] and teacher George DeJong to facilitate trips to the lands of the Bible

(Egypt, Jordan, and Israel—where I grew to love the older Testament). In Egypt we visit massive temple structures with pylon gates more than one hundred feet tall. The bigger the gates (or the bigger the statue), the bigger their god. Pieces of gigantic sculptures have been unearthed where a shoulder alone of the granite statue of Ramesses II at the Ramesseum spans more than six feet. The people at that time believed their gods were so big that no one could escape their presence. So when the psalmist David wrote (hundreds of years after the construction of the Egyptian temples), "Lift up your heads, O gates! And lift them up, O ancient doors, that the King of glory may come in,"[62] it takes on a different meaning. Our God, our King of glory is so big, even colossal gates and doors must be lifted for His entrance. They just aren't high enough.

Our prayers in the valley reveal how big we believe our God to be. After Jesus calmed the sea, the Text says the disciples "were filled with great fear and said to one another, 'Who then is this, that even the wind and the sea obey Him?'"[63] The disciples already saw Jesus turn water into wine and give sight to the blind, but the sea was the abyss and represented chaos for desert people. Now they witnessed His power over that too. Jesus' authority was expanding in their eyes, and they were in awe.

What we believe is true about Jesus and what we believe is true about His Word will greatly influence every part of our lives. And when we experience this truth, it dramatically changes how and why we do what we do. I'm sad to say my prayers when stumbling through a valley often revert to desperation not faith. I question if God knows my troubles, and in doubt I regularly take back the reigns. My default is to ask the Lord to bless my efforts instead of choosing to shadow Him. To pray He goes along with my amazing ideas rather than inquire as to what He wants to do. Which is like playing on a team with André and never passing him the ball. He is with me on the court but I'm not allowing Him to be involved. I am ignoring the best player on the team, the one who can change the game. I need to *dare* pass Jesus the ball and let Him control the outcome. I need to *dare* believe God is way bigger than I think He is, especially in the valley.

When Joshua led the Israelite army to battle against the Amorites in a valley near Gibeon, he *dared* to ask God for the sun to stand still until the nation avenged itself on its enemies.[64] That is some serious hutzpah. One might surmise his experience with Moses in Rephidim may have increased his confidence in the enormous power of God. What if while struggling in our valley, we knew the Lord would provide whatever we need to make it through? Would it change how we pray? What if we woke up each day intent to pursue what we were incapable of accomplishing without divine intervention?

> I want to pray like God is *big*!
> I want to pray for miracles.
> I want to *dare* appear silly in my prayers.
> I want my valley to be a place of victory.

The Lord's exclusive plan for each of our lives will be impossible to bring about in our own strength. That is how we know it's His plan. We need Him and we need community. A vision attainable without God will be limited by our own humanness. I want to be part of something bigger than what I can achieve, to believe in the impossible, to *dare* pray gigantic prayers and rest my faith in a really *big* God!

As I write, I am seated on a plane next to a guy who has completed fifteen, one-hundred-mile runs across the globe. I didn't even know that was a thing. The thought of one such race is staggering, and fifteen is unthinkable. He said it takes him seventeen-to-thirty hours to finish an ultra-marathon depending on terrain. Before he purpose-fully enters that valley, he needs to run and run and then run some more. And when that's done, he goes and runs again. The completion of each ultra-marathon makes a runner better equipped to enter the next one.

As we experience God's unexpected strength in valleys that feel like one-hundred-mile runs, we learn how to persevere *with* Him. A presence-directed relationship with the Lord will increase our faith the more we pursue it. It will equip and prepare us for what is to come. And as we traverse valley after valley, empowered by the Holy Spirit, the next one is a little less taxing.

Our daily journey to struggle together *with* the Lord—where He has marked the path through prolonged valleys comprised of shat-tered dreams, disappointments, or a world-wide pandemic—will infuse us with His comforting peace and incredible power. And along the way we will discover He never abandons us, His love never ceases, and His mercies are new every morning.[65] Trusting the Lord to be with us in the valley may not change the storm, but it will change us. So I will *dare* to choose Jesus. Again, and again. In my tears. In my heartache. In my brokenness. For those who hope in the Lord will not be disappointed.[66]

Chapter 8

THE WAITING ROOM

Seven years had elapsed since the Holy Spirit spoke to my heart, and the absence of men created a palpable void. I longed for companionship and an escape from a constant stream of estrogen. But for now, romance remained off the table. My wait-ability (in a seemingly endless stretch) made me question whether God saw my prime slipping away. Nearing forty, the possibility of having children faded with every passing year. I desperately wanted the Lord to orchestrate His plan, to open Mitch's eyes, to somehow bring us together, but from my vantage point I saw no headway.

My resolve to wait, regrettably, didn't stop phone calls and well-meaning attempts to connect me with brothers, friends, or the single guy at church. Once, a ruggedly handsome man showed up at my door asking for a date. His kind heart, love for Jesus, dimples, and sparkling blue eyes made saying no one of the more difficult choices in this waiting room. I fought putting my life on hold to trust what I couldn't see and struggled to fight *with* God not *against* Him. I missed the excitement of dating and the feeling of being special to someone. Even a few close but unhealthy friendships dissolved. My familiar no longer looked recognizable.

When I first started this journey, the smallest storm threatened to steer me off course, rattling my emotions and intensifying my doubt.

And often it worked. But now after seven years, valleys were rare. I had entered a silent pause: a time of waiting. And in this stillness the Lord spoke these words to my heart, *I have a plan for your life. I know who you are going to marry. I know when it will happen and how it will unfold. Until then, I want you to wait.*

"Wait?" I responded. "Don't you mean date?"

"No. Just wait."

The Leisure of God

Our time-driven society has made us slaves to the clock and our calendar. The demands of work, family, and responsibilities train us to believe it is the movement itself that matters. The preferred answer to "How are you?" is "I'm really busy." Regularly, that has been my reply. As if being busy were some sort of badge I had finally attained. Between doing what I needed and doing what I loved, I resembled a hamster on a wheel running for the sake of movement but not getting anywhere.

I remember a popular television show welcoming a special guest to a stage containing two rows of ten slender poles all fastened to the floor. The guest proceeded to take a china plate, center it on the point of a stick, and give it a whirl. One after another, he twirled a plate on the top of a pole then ran, grabbed another plate, and headed to the next one. As more dishes gyrated on the tip of their sticks, the speed necessary to keep them all spinning increased. I felt frantic just watching. The teetering, the running, the replacing of a plate when one fell and shattered. Finally, all the plates whirled in unison. This moment of bliss—the goal of all his striving—lasted only seconds before each plate began to topple and fall.

We hastily attempt to balance the schedule of our lives with the same tenacity. Yet after expending substantial effort, we have hardly enough time to enjoy the brevity of our success (or the treasure of relationships) before we get drawn into the next round of frenzy. Rare are the days of no agenda and no alarm clock. Even our vacations become filled with activities that drain our energy rather than rejuvenate us. We are losing our ability to slow down and be still. We are losing our ability to wait.

When we stop to think about it, we spend much of our lives in a waiting room. Waiting for Christmas, waiting for summer vacation, waiting for graduation, waiting for healing, waiting for restoration, waiting for marriage, waiting to become pregnant, waiting for _____ (fill in the blank). We spend five years of our lives just waiting in line somewhere and nearly six months of that is at traffic lights.[67] While no one can escape having to wait, I wonder how many of us wait well?

One summer I took a break from coaching to spend five weeks traveling through South America playing basketball for Athletes in Action.[68] Our team was comprised of current and former Division I athletes from across the United States. Except for a blistering run-in with the Brazilian Olympic team, we had an incredible experience. You'd think the culture and language barrier would have created the greatest dissonance, but for me it was the schedule. Or should I say the lack of one. We had daily games to play and flights to catch, but the laidback Latin Americans embodied a different sense of time, which, despite my Puerto Rican ancestry, left me frustrated.

We typically pulled into an arena an hour before the game to crowds that had gathered to watch a team with a few tall blonde Americans play a familiar sport. The stands filled, the officials, coaches, and opposing team were all in the gym, yet no one seemed in a hurry for tip off. Nationals and participants happily hung out with us in the bleachers, talking and laughing, until two hours *after* our scheduled game time, when they decided we should play. It took weeks for me to adapt to the timelessness of their way of life.

Waiting to me feels like a waste. So much can be accomplished in only thirty minutes. Unexpected delays war against my internal clock and battle my to-do list where margins are almost indistinguishable. I quickly become irritated and critical when the completion of a task falls behind schedule. (Yeah, not one of my better traits.)

In my quest to save "valuable" time, I search for the shortest checkout line at the grocery store, turn the stove on high to hasten cooking time, and during conversations mentally formulate what I want to say as I feign listening. I pop bread out of the toaster just to see if it's done, and seldom wait for the second panel of a revolving door. A multitasker at heart, I keep several open windows routinely scattered across my computer screen. I even amassed enough speeding tickets while recruiting as a college coach, that I nearly had my license suspended. (I prefer not to have to follow someone's bumper when up ahead lies an open road.)

This current waiting room was destroying my life plan.

Waiting well takes patience, and patience is an agonizing virtue to develop. Like a muscle, it requires targeted discomfort to grow into something beautiful. Having enough intestinal fortitude to wait something out in itself is not patience. Just because we endure for a specified time doesn't mean we are waiting well. Patiently waiting is waiting with hope, waiting with a peaceful heart, waiting with joyful anticipation, waiting in expectant faith. And the only way we can learn to wait well is by consciously giving control of our lives back to the Lord and changing our mindset. The prayer "Lord, give me patience, and I want it now" sadly doesn't work at all. I've tried it.

This side of heaven, we will never fully grasp the leisure of God's timing or the reasoning behind His thoughts. God's ways just aren't ours.[69] He allowed His own chosen people to be enslaved in Egypt for four hundred years because the iniquity of the Amorites (the people currently living in the promised land) was not yet complete.[70] I don't know about you, but I wouldn't think it all that great to be kept in bondage while the Lord waited on other people. He certainly could have found a more efficient way to accomplish the same thing.

While it may sound strange, I gained a humbling new perspective in the silence of my wait as I worked on counted cross-stitch designs. Cross-stitch is a type of hand embroidery that uses x-shaped stitches and a tiled pattern to create an image on a blank piece of material counting squares as you go. With my limited budget, counted cross-stitch gifts were inexpensive yet meaningful. Although some patterns took just days to finish and others needed months, the result delighted the recipient.

As a novice trying to complete the project as fast as I could (not a surprise, I know), I wouldn't take the time to tie off the various strands when I could just pull the thread across the back to the next location in the pattern that required the same color. As a result, the back side of my cross-stitch didn't look anything like the finished product. Threads intertwined with each other with no semblance of order or reason. I found it impossible to grasp meaning from the path of seemingly random colors by looking at the tangled mess on the back. The front side, however, revealed the beauty of the design.

For a visual learner like me, those projects helped me realize that much of my life I will never comprehend. My finite understanding of an infinite God is like trying to grasp His thoughts or ways by looking at the underside of a novice tapestry. We have no clue why threads crisscross all over the place or why the whole process takes so long. We lack the knowledge of why certain colors must be stitched first or that additional embellishments take time. Our continued and limited view of the back side gives rise to frustration.

But the Lord sees what we cannot, and He is never in a hurry to finish His work. He created the original pattern and meticulously puts in place each thread. He knows exactly how long it will take to complete what He designed and the perfection that will result. As we seek out His instruction manual and continue to persevere through ordinary days, we will feel compelled to release our agendas even when we don't know the outcomes. The more we learn to trust what we cannot see and rely on the timing of His plan, the more our relationship with the Lord deepens.

Surrendering My Agenda

For the most part, I would describe myself as low maintenance. I require little to be content, and accumulating things has never been important to me. However, when I *really* want something, I want it *now* and I want my plans to progress exactly as I think they should. The smallest change to my agenda unsettles me.

Now in my seventh year of waiting, I started to receive mixed signals from Mitch. Occasionally, when we ran into each other, he would hold me in a lengthy hug, walk me to my car as I left a function, or tenderly lean his head against mine. While appreciated and welcomed, his actions felt confusing since I knew he was dating at the time. But after living in this waiting room for years, I also knew my attempts to accomplish God's will in my own power or to sprint out ahead of Him to speed up His call on my life would fail. I had learned (through painful experience) those efforts only made things worse, my heart took a beating, and the Lord would inevitably have to lead me back home. So I relinquished my agenda and continued to wait.

Alone, in this quiet space I desperately needed the strength of the Lord to carry on. There was no way I could gut this one out. *My* goals, *my* plans, and *my* agendas faded away as my desires took a back seat. In those moments of surrender, Jesus' loving hands surrounded my breaking heart, and His gentleness reassured my soul. *My strength will be enough*, He told me. *Learn to recognize My voice and follow. I am preparing you for what is to come.*

Jesus eradicated my autonomy and taught me to lean on Him. At times when the ache seemed poised to take me down, His Word to my spirit would lift me back up; its resonating truth piercing the emotions that threatened to derail the wait. Nights and weekends, normally occupied by dating, I now spent pouring the Word into my soul. I attended women's events and marriage conferences and read books on how to be a good wife. Anything to keep my eyes focused on the Lord and off the wait. Whenever my potential husband chose to follow the Lord and move toward me, I wanted to do my best to be ready. Hope for the future grew. My love and passion for music also flourished during this time, and I returned to the recording studio to complete a second album titled, *My Father, My Friend*. And Jesus was becoming just that. My Friend. I felt His grace pour into my spirit with every pursuit to *know* Him, not just know *about* Him. The more time passed, the more my heart craved His presence and required His power to keep holding on.

Stay the Course

Once freed from the slavery of the Egyptians, the Israelites still doubted the Lord was big enough to successfully lead them to conquer the land of promise. They inevitably ended up in their own waiting room where, for forty years, they had to learn to rely on God's faithful provision and protection. Following the death of Moses, the Lord reassured His people and their newly appointed leader, Joshua, of His continual presence: "Moses my servant is dead. Now therefore arise, go over this Jordan … just as I was with Moses, so I will be with you. I will not leave you or forsake you."[71] God promised Joshua and the Israelites that He would never abandon them, that He would guide them into Canaan. And after forty years of waiting, they stood ready to follow.

Strengthened by the presence of the Lord and His direction to enter a new land, Joshua instructed the priests to step into the Jordan River with the ark of the covenant. It sounds like a simple command, but at the time of their crossing, the river would have been at flood stage. The priests had to *dare* to trust the Lord to walk into the raging water carrying the ark. Once they stepped in, the Text says God miraculously stopped the water from flowing by piling it up at Adam, nearly eighteen miles upriver.[72]

The details are unknown. All the water from Jericho to Adam could have instantly evaporated or reversed its flow to dry out the riverbed. Or it could be that when the Lord stopped the river at Adam, eighteen miles worth of water may have had to pass by the priests before the Israelite nation could cross. And the priests would have had to stand in the water until it did.

On average, rivers flow from three-to-six miles per hour, which would require the priests to stand in the overflowing Jordan anywhere from three-to-six hours before the eighteen miles of turbulent water would abate. That's a long time to stand in a river with or without a current. While this entire idea may be a stretch, it speaks to me. Waiting in faith for us might mean the surging water has eighteen more miles to go and we need to stand for a while, or the water has reached mile nine and deliverance is on its way, or the culmination of the chaos is just around the bend and backing out now ruins everything.

The priests chose to follow the Lord into the river, but they had no idea how hard it would be or when it would end. "Be strong and courageous. Do not be frightened, and do not be dismayed, for the Lord your God is with you wherever you go"[73] became their hope, and it needs to become ours. Expect to feel fear in the wait. Just don't run away or become disheartened because of it. Standing in faith—when the end seems nowhere in sight—is the very definition of courageous.

Right now, you may be alone in your waiting room, wondering when God will move and feeling unsure if you have the strength to hold out. You are weary, exhausted, and yearning for encouragement. You want to bail. No one understands, and those who want to, struggle to find words that speak to your heart.

But as we remain faithful, the day will come when we realize in our bones that His power enabled us to stay the course. His power showed itself strong when we were at our weakest and had nothing left.

I feel inspired to persevere when I read of those in the Bible who *dared* to stand in faith for decades, who *dared* to believe the Lord despite trying circumstances. The improbable men and women of faith listed in chapter 11 of Hebrews *dared* to believe they would have descendants to number the stars and that one day their people would return to a land of promise. It is an incredible passage of astonishing faith. But when we consider the length of each of their lives (some lasting hundreds of years), their big faith moment, taking up only a verse or two, is barely a nanosecond in the measure of time. Little mention is made of how they grappled with the angst of their wait or how, day after day, they stood in faith believing and seeing nothing.

Abram was seventy-five when God made a covenant with him that he would be the father of many nations, and at age one hundred, Isaac (the son of the promise) was born. What did Abram do for twenty-five years? How did he stay faithful? Large spans of time pass between

Bible verses with barely a mention. Noah received directions to build an ark sometime after he turned five hundred years old, and he was six hundred when the flood came. Estimates suggest that it took anywhere from fifty-five to seventy-five years to build the ark.[74]

How did Noah handle the ridicule, the doubt, the workload, the struggle? How did he stay the course when the days and years dragged on? How do we?

Luke tells the story in the beginning of his Gospel of a priest named Zechariah, who along with his wife, Elizabeth, were well along in years and had no children.[75] Early in their marriage, they must have pleaded with the Lord for a child. Now older, I doubt they persisted in that prayer. Zechariah, a man of the Text, would have known a miracle pregnancy later in life happened only once before—with the patriarch Abraham and his wife, Sarah. He probably deemed himself unworthy of something similar, and with Elizabeth, had resigned themselves to being childless. Their prayers were *more* likely for the Messiah to come and deliver His people. So when the angel Gabriel showed up in the temple announcing that the long-awaited answer to their petitions as a young couple would finally be revealed through the birth of their son, John, Zechariah justifiably responded with disbelief.

Not long after Zechariah encountered Gabriel, a young girl named Mary also had a divine visitation foretelling an event totally impossible from a human standpoint. Despite the improbability of giving birth without ever knowing a man, Mary *dared* to believe God would fulfill His words to her. Devoid of fanfare, yet the recipient of ample judgment and rejection, Mary became the mother of Jesus. But it was years before her little boy chose to reveal He was the long-awaited Messiah. And during that waiting room, Mary continued to train up Jesus in the way He should go. God's plan for restoration didn't culminate with the birth of Jesus, that's where it took another turn.

Jesus, in His own thirty-year waiting room, learned patience and submission from His parents while preparing for His three-and-a-half-year ministry. (Not our seminarians. They endure three-and-a-half years of training to serve in ministry for thirty.) But Jesus knew Who He was, and why He was here. His intimate relationship with the Father gave Him confidence to walk the road of service. In His obedience and in the wait, He grew. We do too. As the prophet Isaiah reminds us, "They who wait for the Lord shall renew their strength; they shall mount up with wings like eagles; they shall run and not be weary; they shall walk and not faint."[76] As we stay the course in our waiting room, the Lord will empower us for every situation we face. And in our silent pause, we open the door for God to do a work in us, just as He did with Jesus.

Plant Seeds

No one prays for a waiting room any more than they would pray for suffering. Probably because waiting requires a dependence on someone other than ourselves and a spirit that is humble enough to give up control. If we want to experience the amazing process of transformation (like one of junior chef to master chef, or caterpillar to butterfly) it only happens there. But time alone isn't all it takes for change. Waiting involves effort. It requires an investment, a planting of what might be considered ordinary that grows into something extraordinary.

I have always been an easy mark for a young person showing up at my door selling just about anything for a school fundraiser. One fall afternoon it was tulip bulbs. I excitedly picked out a variety of colors and, as a gardening rookie, made sure to follow the directions. I dug holes, poured in water, planted the small bulbs, pressed firmly to remove air pockets, and watered some more. Then I waited. Tulip bulbs are planted in the fall because they need the cold winter soil to flower the following spring. And seven months later, tulips, exactly what I planted, broke through the ground with delightful beauty.

Little by little, I am learning whatever seeds I choose to plant in my life will one day bear fruit. Will they be seeds of hope, trust, honesty, and love? Or seeds of doubt, fear, duplicity, and anger? Eventually we are going to reap whatever it is that we have sown. If the seed we plant is good—whether it is a personality trait or a habit—we must nurture it with the expectation of a future harvest. If we don't like the seed, we need to stop planting it. And if we don't like what's starting to grow, we need to pull it out. As a friend often tells me, we must feed what we want to live and starve what we want to die. What we plant and nourish is reflected by the fruit that is evident in the character of our lives while we wait.

I *dare* to believe it is worthwhile to sow in areas where I desire my life to be different, where I want to see the fruit of positive change. To remain loyal to reap devoted friends. To attend wedding showers and support ministries that value godly marriages, so one day my own marriage will realize the benefits. To invest in young people, believing others will do the same should I have my own kids. To care for relatives as they age, so when the time comes, loving provision will be returned.

In my quest to harvest good fruit during a season of waiting, I plant seeds of patience and compassion by standing in the long lines, slowing down to let other cars merge, and sending hope-filled notes when I feel disheartened. When I recognize a personal void, I invest my time, passion, and resources in that area. "For where your treasure is, there your heart will be also."[77]

To keep from becoming discouraged, I daily list at least two things I am grateful for and make a concerted effort to consistently exercise both my mind and my body. If I want the fruit of contentment to grow in my heart, I look up verses on contentment and do a word study until that seed begins to produce full-grown fruit. If fear dominates my thought life, I find verses on faith and post them around my home to meditate on the Lord's promises. When I become too self-absorbed, I turn into a "wait-er" and step up to serve. And should I be treated poorly, I try to respond with kindness (although not always successfully) and trust the Lord to one day do a work in their hearts. I have made a conscious choice to keep planting in places I want to reap, *daring* to believe—after a few long, cold winters—there will be a bountiful harvest.

Developing an intimate relationship with Jesus is a gradual process too (as it is with most relationships). We must be willing to press in over time, even when life is difficult. Not long ago a friend showed me a rock that carried on it the imprint of a shell. For that imprint to have been made, the stone and the shell were pressed together for a long time. If I want to reflect Jesus well, on the inside and on the outside, I need to press into Him and stay there, even when what I see is far from encouraging.

During any lengthy growing process when it seems nothing is happening, the temptation to give up is very real. Trusting God to reveal His plan in His timing requires years where, like a farmer waiting for the crop, it feels all we are doing is getting in and out of bed. And then the next day we get up and go to bed, and the next, and the next, and the next. As Jesus reminds us, "The kingdom of God is as if a man should scatter seed on the ground. He sleeps and rises night and day, and the seed sprouts and grows; he knows not how."[78] Years may pass between the planting of our seeds and the harvest. And during the in-between days, it will appear as if nothing is stirring, nothing is transpiring. Hold on. Stay the course. Don't give up. The water will subside, the fruit will come, an answer is on its way.

One of my favorite quotes is by author Ann Kiemel Anderson who wrote, "It is how you live your ordinary days that determines whether or not you have big moments."[79] There is a whole lot of getting up and going to bed during ordinary days when it feels as if we are watching grass grow. In our passionate pursuit of a dream, we must continue to put one foot in front of the other, pour into people, serve, and press into Jesus. Even when no fruit is visible.

Be encouraged, friend, we are not the only ones sowing seeds! As a follower of Jesus Christ, the seed of the Holy Spirit has been divinely planted into our spirits, deeply rooting all that He is into our hearts. And when we choose to stay the course, He will produce in us the fruit of love, joy, peace, patience, kindness, goodness, faithfulness, gentleness, and self-control.[80]

As we cultivate what He has planted with the water of the Word, obedience, and with faith-filled prayer, we can expect the Lord will produce in us, for us, and through us an abundant harvest.

So, as a dedicated farmer waits for his crop, keep *getting up and going to bed* even in the absence of progress. In the wait, plant good seeds, water them well, and press into Jesus. Desire His intimate embrace more than His promise, knowing that He remains on the throne even when we are in a silent pause. Trust that when all human reason for hope is gone, *daring* faith is still possible. Exactly what God authored, planned, wrote out, and placed in our hearts He will bring to pass in His time. "And let us not grow weary of doing good, for in due season we will reap, if we do not give up."[81]

I am still not great at waiting ... but I *am* getting better.

Chapter 9

ARE YOU IN THE HOUSE?

During what felt like a lengthy, drawn-out waiting period, my daily challenge was to stay still. To listen and wait for the Lord to lead. I really wanted to change Mitch's heart, to make him want to pursue a relationship with me. But I tried that already and it only made things worse. It didn't help to insert my life into his or to conjure up ways to cross paths. Although I resisted the urge to ask him out, the past eight years produced no visible fruit in the relationship department. And I remained helpless to do anything to speed up the process.

Some days felt easy to navigate, others not so much. My confidence wavered as I fluctuated from intense anger to *daring* faith. Then came the days I simply wanted to bail on hard and run home to Mom and Dad. Maybe you know the feeling.

For me, thoughts of *home* warm my heart and draw me in. Mostly due to family. I still drive by houses where we used to live vividly recalling the laughs, the puppies, the tree forts, and the crack in the driveway that marked the free throw line. But home is not always so idyllic and—like a visiting team playing on their opponent's home court—we aim to get out of the "house" as soon as possible.

As a young girl I readily dreamt of leaving home to venture out on my own. I imagined the delight in never having to do chores or share a bedroom. I could watch a show past 8:00 p.m., sleep in 'til noon, and eat ice cream for breakfast. What a life! But without a job, a driver's license, or an ability to cook (I still struggle there), I'd have been grossly unprepared to step into that reality. Not to mention I would have *really* missed my family.

It's hard to leave home when we aren't ready; to break the unique bond designed to exist within a family. Even though the composition of family has changed over the years and the traditional Christmas photo now includes the dog, whatever our families look like or wherever they settle, it becomes home.

Home for me has been a parsonage, an apartment, a house, a tent, even manufactured housing. But no matter my residence, it became a space where laughter invaded, dreams were birthed, and stepping out in faith valued and encouraged. Home remained a safe place to *dare.* When my efforts fell short (which happened more often than I would have liked), the secure love of family urged me to get back up, dust myself off, and try again.

My eagerness to grow up, coupled with an unrestrained confidence, caused me to step into areas I wasn't ready for. I vividly remember being rescued after diving into the deep end of the pool and my epic fail at controlling a room of six-year-olds during my first substitute teaching assignment. (Give me teenagers any day!)

When visions are not yet real in our lives, our attempts to step in and fulfill God's call hinders us from being truly present and at home with the Lord. Our gaze—once fixed on Him—turns inward and we lose the path. Although vision propels us forward, it also forms in us a desire to move out ahead of God, and the result is a tangible separation. His transformation in our lives then hits a wall and we need to return home.

Come Home

The Bible portrays similar struggles in those we consider giants of the faith. Abram, Joseph, and Moses were aware of God's call on their lives and each of them attempted to step forward in their vision before it was time.

God promised Abram that one day his descendants would number the stars in the sky,[82] and he believed it. However, after an eleven-year wait and still no kids, Abram (at eighty-six years of age) took matters into his own hands and fathered Ishmael with someone other than his wife. But Ishmael wasn't the son of the promise, and Abram had to wait another fourteen years before Sarah would miraculously give birth to Isaac. Abram tried to step into his call ahead of God and ended up needing to return to place his trust in the Lord.[83] He had to come home.

Joseph, in his youthfulness, eagerly told his brothers of his dream: that one day they would all bow down before him.[84] Clearly his older brothers took offense at the thought. Most would. Joseph was already Dad's favorite, and hearing his dream only made his brothers hate him more. The absence of love among the boys was undeniable. Following a second dream portraying his upcoming fame, Joseph bragged about it to the entire family, including his father. Jealousy and anger seethed among the clan and at the next available opportunity, the brothers sold him into slavery and told their father he was dead. For the next thirteen years (some of those spent in prison) the Lord shaped Joseph. A desire to fulfill the vision had prompted Joseph to action, but it wasn't yet time for him to rule.

Moses wasn't much different. Born a Hebrew, the Lord saved him from infanticide and steered (literally) his adoption by Pharaoh's daughter. For years he grew up enjoying the wealth and privilege that came with living in the palace. But Moses knew his heritage, and deep within his spirit the Lord had planted a seed, a knowing, that one day he would deliver God's enslaved people. The seed, however, had not yet matured when in a moment of rage, he killed an Egyptian who beat a Hebrew slave. Moses tried to step into his call outside of God's timing and ended up having to escape the Egyptians' fury by holing up in the land of Midian for forty years.[85]

How many of us have jumped ahead of the Lord and left the safety and care of His house? How many of us, with a dream in our hearts, took off in a full sprint, glancing occasionally over our shoulders and praying the Lord would keep up? Clearly, we are not designed to stay at home forever, but running out ahead of God creates a myriad of problems, some with unintended consequences.

Jesus tells a story of a young man who struggled with being home. Although integral to the family business, the youngest of two sons longed to be free from responsibility. He felt trapped living with his parents. One day he told his father as much and requested his portion of the inheritance. Surprisingly, his father consented, and the son left to fulfil his dreams, money in hand.[86] If you aren't familiar with this narrative, you can probably guess what happened. It wasn't long before the young man's cash dried up, his so-called friends disappeared, and he found himself digging through trash just to eat. He pondered his dismal state, *My father's servants have plenty of bread, and I am dying of hunger. Maybe if I go home and agree to work as a hired hand my father will take me back.*[87] The son's desire for home—for acceptance, for safety, for what was familiar—drew him back in. On his return journey he rehearsed what he would say to his father to appease the expected anger and disappointment.

As the family estate came into view, the son saw a figure running toward him. It was his father! Fearful, the young man quickly began to recite his canned speech, hoping to suppress an outburst. His father, filled with compassion, barely let him say a word before he fell onto his neck, kissed him, and called for a celebration.

His son was back in the house.

His son was home.

Our heavenly Father created each one of us for relationship with Him, to be in His house. And we often run away. He knows that when we fix our eyes on Jesus and chase after His heart, the things of this earth will fade into the background. But it requires more than just being present.

Be There

Many have skillfully perfected the art of being in the house and not being there at the same time. The young man's older brother, upon hearing news that his lost sibling had returned, became indignant at the party his father was throwing in his brother's honor. Ignoring his father's humble request, the eldest son refused to go into the house, appalled that his own faithfulness never resulted in a family celebration.

The father pleaded with his eldest, "Son, you are always with me, and all that is mine is yours."[88] In other words, "You have been in the house and part of our family your entire life. You have access to all the advantages of a first-born—in fact, everything here is yours anyway—but you have rejected the blessings of home."

The older son may have been home, but he was never really there.

We have all fallen into the trap of looking like we were faithfully following the Lord when all along our service was mere image management. Our heart wasn't engaged, and we knew it. We worked in children's ministry then complained about the unruly kids to whomever would listen. We gave to the church then criticized how they spent our money. We attended marriage conferences thinking our spouse might finally get it yet remained unwilling to alter our own behavior. Those actions may satisfy onlookers (and deceive us as well) but the Lord longs for more.

When God told Moses to bring the leading men of Israel to worship Him on the mountain, Moses built an altar and twelve pillars (one for each of the tribes of Israel) at the base of Mount Sinai. Then he, along with Aaron, Nadab, Abihu, and seventy of the elders went up to behold the God of Israel.[89] But there's more. From there, the Lord wanted to take Moses to another level, a deeper experience of His presence, and He told him, "Come up to me on the mountain and wait there, that I may give you the tablets of stone, with the law and the commandment, which I have written for their instruction."[90] As we look closely at differing translations of the first part of Exodus 24:12, we see the Lord was asking something unique of Moses:

> Come up to me on the mountain and *wait* there. (ESV)
> Come up to me into the mount, and *be* there. (KJV)
> Come up to Me on the mountain and *remain* there. (NET)
> Come up to me on the mountain and *stay* here. (NIV)

What did the Lord ask Moses to do? Each statement sounds similar, except for the King James Version, which at first glance appears redundant: "Come up to me into the mount, and *be* there."[91] If Moses went up to the Lord on the mountain, he would already be there. So why say go there *and* be there? If you told a friend, "Meet me at the coffee house and *be* there," they might look at you funny. Words like *wait, remain,* or *stay* make more sense. However, all four of those words were translated from the same Hebrew word, *hayah,* which means to *be.*[92] And though it feels repetitive, *be there* might be just what God meant.

We have all been to a concert, in a meeting, at church, or talking with a long-winded friend on the phone. Although we may have been physically present, we weren't really there. High school students have mastered the ability to mindlessly nod their heads to make teachers think they're paying attention, all the while they are not there.

Social media exacerbates this phenomenon. Rare are the conversations when someone is not checking their phone after every ding, light, or vibration. Various platforms seem to have us working for them rather than the other way around. Many wanting to capture the moment and post it to the cyber world are no longer there but are instead anticipating the likes of those who are not. Although their body is present, they aren't. We feel it. God does too. We need to go back home. And we need to *be there*.

Square One

In *The Renewed Mind*, author Larry Christenson describes himself playing an imaginary table game.

> Each player had a token. Everyone started off on Square 1, but you couldn't move off Square 1 until a little Red Bird came along and sat down on Square 1 while your token was there. Then you could go.
>
> The game got under way. The players moved out and landed on different places at the spin of a dial. Eventually the Red Bird settled down next to me, so I got off Square 1.
>
> Going around the board, you land on some squares where you have to pick up a card from the middle of the table. Every time I picked up one of those cards it told me, *Go Back to Square 1*. Then I had to sit and wait for the little Red Bird to come along again. It was rather frustrating.

I thought about that a bit, musing to myself, *This is a picture of the Christian life.* The Holy Spirit's purpose for me is to get me back to Square 1. And that is His purpose for the church.

The key to living the Christian life is to go back to Square 1, and continually to move out only from Square 1.

What is "Square 1"? That is the place where we cannot do or initiate anything by ourselves. We have to wait for the little Red Bird to come along. We can spin the dial as much as we please, but it does not produce any real progress until the little Red Bird comes along to release us."[93]

Square 1 is home. It is the place where we begin to realize there is no moving ahead in the Christian life on our own if we truly desire to follow God. When given a vision, a call on our lives, we desperately want to move forward, but we must wait for the Holy Spirit to do a work and lead us out. We cannot run our lives by ourselves without creating a mess.

I experienced the frustration of being in the starting blocks for what felt like an eternity, only to sprint out before the gun and be sent back to wait. I tried interjecting myself into Mitch's life and nothing ever moved our relationship forward. Stepping out ahead of God only resulted in continued rejection and the need to return to Square 1 and wait.

Mitch wasn't the only relationship I tried to accelerate outside of God's timing. It extended to other people too. In my excitement about the Lord's plan for my life, I was careless. I shared the words the Lord downloaded to my spirit with those who were unable (or unwilling) to grasp the ambiguity of my vision. I shouldn't have been surprised. God told *me* His vision for my life. He didn't tell everyone else. My intentions were pure—I wanted the faith of my friends to increase by seeing this all play out with Mitch—but the exact opposite happened. As years passed, their doubt grew and their faith dwindled. My desire to listen for and to follow what I believed the Lord said to me (especially when it didn't come directly from a verse in the Text) clashed with their theology. In turn, close friends rejected me too. It stung. While I longed for support and encouragement to stay the course, their doubt fueled my own and spending time together felt awkward. They soon walked away, and I humbly returned home.

I still believe we need to share our vision. We must "write the vision; make it plain on tablets, so he may run who reads it."[94] We must invite people into our story as our Aaron and Hur, who will help hold up our arms and support us along the way.[95] We just need to be sure to share our vision with the *right* people.

That's where I blew it. In my excitement, I didn't check with the Lord before I revealed my story. I didn't consider carefully who I told and ended up causing more harm than good. I ran out ahead of God and damaged numerous relationships. The chorus from Kathy Troccoli's song, "A Different Road," reflected my change of heart:

> *So now I'll walk a different road.*
> *I want to see Him there before I even go.*
> *I've run ahead and gone too slow.*
> *I've got to be still now, wait upon His will now.*
> *This time, it's gonna be His time.*[96]

It's not about trying to accomplish our own vision. We need to show up and be present on Square 1 and offer the Lord all we have, then let Him assume responsibility for fulfilling His call on our lives. Which is so much easier to say than to do. Some days I felt decisive, *daring* to trust the Lord at any cost, only to succumb to doubt the following day. And while at certain moments it seemed my faith could move mountains, I repeatedly struggled to wait for the Lord and not move out in my own strength; to be good at staying with Him in the house until He said, *It's time.* Some days I white-knuckled the furniture just to keep from running away from home to birth an Ishmael.

Maybe you have left home or never fully accepted what God is offering. Maybe you have tried to make a relationship work or forced yourself into someone else's business. Maybe you have pushed a sale too hard or coerced your kids to accomplish your dreams. Maybe while feeling the pressure of limited finances, you found a way to make ends meet that crossed an ethical line. You stepped out ahead of God.

Saying yes to Jesus is saying yes to the only One who knows you best, the only One who wants to *be* at home with you no matter what you've done. It is *daring* to say yes to His timing. It is *daring* in faith to believe first and understand later. And it all starts by choosing to be present in His house and expecting His presence to change you. For from that place, the Lord will instill in you the courage to follow the Holy Spirit off Square 1 and into the glory of His vision, even when what you see is disheartening.

Don't Believe What You See

As the disciples followed Jesus throughout Galilee, what they saw—an ill Roman servant, a raging storm, the death of a nobleman's daughter, blind men, a man controlled by an unclean spirit, a woman with an issue of blood, and a widow's dead son—appeared impossible to overcome.[97] But visible facts never hindered Jesus.

On one such occasion, thousands of people pressed in close to hear Jesus. Captivated for hours by His teaching and His presence, the large crowd began to get hungry. The disciples suggested He send the people into the surrounding countryside and villages so they could buy themselves some food. Jesus, however, responded to the disciples with, "You give them something to eat."[98] The disciples had just described to Jesus unmanageable circumstances with no visible solution. Yet it was as if Jesus was saying, *You do it. You have been with Me for a while now. You could have spoken to the storm when we were in the boat, and you didn't. Here's another opportunity. You feed them now.*

The disciples had experienced His presence, they were in His house, but the revelation of Jesus had not yet taken root in their hearts. They weren't ready to step into His vision for them. So Jesus demonstrated how to ignore the facts ransacking their thoughts. He looked up to heaven, to His home, said a blessing, and with five loaves and two fish made an enormous meal. Jesus defied the obvious by looking up.

In the third year of His ministry, Jesus arrived in Bethany, where His friends Mary and Martha were mourning the death of their brother, Lazarus.[99] The facts were, Lazarus had been dead four days and a large rock stood in front of the tomb. A burial chamber would have been enough to stop most of us; now add a large stone, objections from the crowd, and certain death. Facts. But Jesus came to the tomb and lifted His eyes. He ignored the mess, the smell, and those who tried to hold Him back. Looking away from the obvious He redirected His focus toward home.

Jesus saw things differently.

He understood that tapping into the power of God forces the evil one to run. Resisting the devil, submitting to God, and standing in truth, will also change what we see. God's truth doesn't rest in our answer to, *What do our eyes see? What are the facts?* or *What do we feel?* Prolonged periods of time spent with the Lord in His house, on Square 1, will lift our eyes to the truth of His promise, enlarging our faith to *dare* disregard what we feel, to *dare* do what is right at the risk of our jobs, to *dare* endure criticism, and to *dare* step forward when others walk away.

To *dare* see things differently.

We may attend church every Sunday, but until we embrace truth, until we *dare* have faith in the greatness of our God, we put our trust in facts. Facts, however, are not always proven valid (which blows my mathematical mind). It's a fact that my spine was so curved doctors recommended rods to correct it—yet God made me an athlete anyway. It's a fact that I broke my wrist—yet still played softball. It's a fact that a young man in our home came under the influence of the evil one— yet Jesus showed Himself more powerful. It's a fact that we can't see Jesus—yet He will pursue us, guide us, restore us, and love us more than anyone else we know.

To prevent myself from being swayed by what I see and feel, I must consciously and intentionally redirect my gaze away from facts and circumstances. Like Jesus, I need to lift my eyes beyond what is visible to see His enduring love for me, to see relationships restored, to see loved ones come to Christ, to see a physical healing, to see my financial situation improve, and to see the truth of the BIG-ness of God. Just one fish and half a loaf, along with a mustard seed-sized faith, will open the door for the Lord to accomplish a mighty work in our lives. And the more we choose to be present in the Lord's house, the more we are empowered with courage to *dare* believe His truth rather than what we see.

Our Final Home

Before the Lord ever spoke the words that altered my life, Dad faced health challenges. He and Mom had long been aware of the vision I held for eight years and provided welcomed advice and prayer support throughout my journey. As Dad's physical condition declined, Mitch again came up in conversation.

Dad was a faith-filled, caring man who didn't waste words. I loved to glean from his wisdom, so I asked, "After all these years, what can you share with me regarding the call of the Lord on my life, the vision I heard from Him?"

"I believe the Spirit has spoken to your heart." Dad replied. "But Terri, when God gives you a vision, death to the vision must occur first. You may even experience a double death."

His words gave me great pause as a sick feeling formed in the pit of my stomach. I remember hearing this idea at a conference with my parents a long time ago. It didn't sound encouraging then either. Death to a vision is derived from the premise that God often leads us to a point where the vision or dream we hold appears dead. Impossible. Done. We see no visible way for it to be realized or resurrected. Dad referenced stories throughout the Bible—Abram, Ruth, Esther, the Samaritan woman, Peter, Paul—people who faced situations that appeared lifeless where the only thing left for them to do was trust the Lord to fulfill His plan.

Dad warned me that fear would rear its ugly head when death to my vision comes. And it's all part of living in *daring* faith. I should expect it. Yes, death to a vision can at times be permanent and it's also necessary for God to bring the vision back to life in a similar yet altogether different manner than we imagined. It is a necessary process. For when our vision dies, we, often by default, turn back to the Lord. And in those moments of heart-rending relinquishment, we begin to discover how to trust the Lord like never before.

I heard what Dad said, still the thought of a double death remained unnerving. No way did I want to experience it twice.

A month after that conversation with Dad, I was surprised to see Mitch at my front door. I excitedly welcomed him in and was surprised again when he greeted me with a warm embrace and a kiss on the cheek. Looking at his face, I knew something was up. Normally an outgoing and cheerful guy, Mitch appeared much more contemplative.

"I just came from seeing your mom and dad," he said.

Yet another surprise.

"Your dad invited me over to talk." Since my parents knew Mitch years before I met him, and with Dad now nearing death, the get together didn't seem unusual. Mitch shared how Dad and Mom told him they believed God had placed a special anointing on his life. "Then your dad gave me permission to date you."

Stunned at this turn of events, and with a wildly beating heart, I asked, "What do you think about Dad's comment to you?"

Mitch offered a coy smile. "I told him it probably wouldn't happen right now."

Although the exchange between Mitch and my parents and his conversation with me at my house caught me totally unaware, it infused my soul with hope and energized my faith. If Mitch hadn't considered a relationship with me before, he could no longer ignore the thought. Maybe this was the spark needed to ignite the fire.

Three days after that conversation Dad died. My heart became laden with grief. God graciously provided Dad with many treasured final moments to express his love and share his faith with those he held dear. And now he had entered his new eternal home.

Home.

Not the place they deliver our mail. Rather the Home that will comfort us in ways we will never find on earth, no matter how hard we look. Our souls are tenderly fashioned to be in relationship with Jesus and nothing else will come close to meeting that need. Not family, not things, not success, not money, not friends, not power, not marriage, not children. We will only be fulfilled when we are truly Home.

That's where I want to be. In His house, both now and forever. For I've learned that as we return to the safety of home and turn our eyes upon Jesus, He will assume the responsibility to fulfill His call on our lives. For it is in this *daring* space that He earns our trust, and we grow to love His heart.

Chapter 10

PURIFY MY HEART

The ebb and flow of my emotional state stabilized with every passing year. Waves of doubt no longer surged through my soul on a daily or even a weekly basis. Even so, moments surfaced when I resembled the father, who, desiring a miracle for his son, cried out to Jesus, "I believe; help my unbelief!"[100] But those instances were rare. Although I saw no evidence of the Lord's plan unfolding, I grew accustomed to believing without seeing, in trusting the Lord with no visible reason for doing so. After mistakenly revealing my vision to those unable to walk this road, I surrounded myself with people of faith who could help me maintain a godly perspective.

In year ten of my wait, I flew to Colorado to visit friends and mentors, John and Terrie Graves. My love for this couple ran deep. We spent the week hiking, target shooting, and traversing picturesque snow-covered mountain ranges with their five kids. In the evenings we would pray together. The night before I left, John and Terrie shared they believed God was taking me through a season of separation and purification. Deep down the words resonated, but I didn't fully grasp what they meant for me. I did recognize, however, that what I once valued—coaching, traveling, attending social events, spending time with friends, or watching the occasional drama series—diminished in importance as my gaze regularly shifted off myself and onto the Lord.

I could only surmise that separation from draining relationships or mindless activities would also enhance God's purification process in my life.

Jumping back into the classroom after a week off proved challenging as I attempted (rather unsuccessfully) to redirect the minds of adolescents to math. When the last student finally exited the room, I collapsed at my desk. A sudden knock on the door jarred me back to reality. Expecting a teenager, I looked up and saw Mitch walking towards me! His refreshing smile and warm embrace quickly dissolved any trace of exhaustion.

Mitch was just returning from a ten-day trip to California and stopped by on his way home to say hello. After describing the welcomed pause from life's routine in much warmer weather than the Midwest, our conversation turned reflective.

"I loved my get away to the West Coast." Mitch said with a smile. "It provided me the space and quiet I needed to listen to the Lord. I can usually hear the Spirit speak to my heart if I am still enough, which is often the problem."

"Well," I asked, "did you hear anything interesting?"

"Yeah, I did. I felt God impress upon my spirit that He was beginning to take me through a season of separation and purification. I'm just not sure what it means."

Did he just say what I think he said? Stunned, I asked him to elaborate.

"If I had to guess, I believe the Lord wants me to sift through the activities I am currently involved in to determine which ones I should eliminate. I need to do a better job of focusing on God and not myself. I imagine that process alone will continue to purify my heart and draw me closer to Him."

Mitch and I were obviously walking a similar road in the same direction, just not together. And in that moment, the Lord again reaffirmed I was right where He wanted me to be.

John and Terrie had challenged me to seek the Lord during this season and to embrace the time of refinement. They also encouraged me to fast and pray. Although my flesh protested (screamed, would be more like it), I purposefully pressed into the purification process and pursued more time alone with Jesus.

I continued my daily responsibilities, still saying yes when asked to serve, but at home my focus shifted. I separated myself from television and social media, became immersed with faith-filled messages and music, read the Word, and fasted for days at a time. During a rather lengthy stint, I grabbed a random cross-stitch project to keep my mind occupied. Weeks later I realized the pattern I followed fittingly produced an intricate cross interlaced with the words of the old hymn, "Standing on the Promises."

> *Standing on the promises of Christ my King.*
> *Through eternal ages let his praises ring.*
> *Glory in the highest, I will shout and sing.*
> *Standing on the promises of God.*
>
> *Standing, standing*
> *Standing on the promises*
> *Of God my Savior*
> *Standing, standing*
> *I'm standing on the promises of God.*[101]

With every stitch that sentiment reverberated through my core.

Over the next year while my relationship with the Lord flourished, my spirit became increasingly disquieted, unsettled. And I couldn't quite articulate why. Standing in faith when what I saw didn't match my vision would naturally elicit trepidation, yet I felt as if something was about to go down.

As though a switch flipped, my relationship with Mitch moved past the friend zone. He sent me a message asking if I would stop by after school to pick up a book and return it to a colleague of mine. When I arrived at his place, he invited me in then walked over to the stereo and hit play.

Soft music flooded the room as he grabbed my hand and pulled me in close. I didn't resist. He must have felt my heart reverberating against his chest as we slow danced across the floor. My feet barely touched the ground. With indescribable delight, I instantly began to picture our future together.

I would love to have kept dancing well into the night, but I was already late for basketball practice and couldn't stay. Sadly, I extricated myself from his embrace and I left his house in a daze. (I'm pretty sure I forgot the book.)

Weeks later, Mitch showed up unexpectedly at my home. As we sat on the couch and caught up on each other's lives, he leaned in and kissed me. Not just once. I felt like the star of my own Hallmark movie! The vision anticipated for more than a decade had come clearly into view.

And then the next day, with little explanation, Mitch said he didn't want to pursue a romantic relationship with me. My heart shattered into a million pieces. I was so confused. As quickly as the door to a future with Mitch opened, it slammed shut.

Daring faith can really hurt.

Maybe you've felt it too. You painstakingly pour yourself into a job or a relationship only to be suddenly rejected at the worst possible time. You study for years to gain acceptance into the college of your choice, and you're blindsided by a pandemic. Is it possible to maintain hope through the humiliating disappointment, the devastating loss, the crushing despair?

Choosing to walk a road of purification and separation is uncomfortable. In fact, it can be downright excruciating. Just hearing the word *purification* creates in me a feeling I'm about to undergo a purging of excess that will be hard, painful, and heart-rending. And separation—I already felt secluded and alone on this journey. For eleven years, I faithfully clung to the words the Lord downloaded to my heart and confirmed in my spirit despite minimal support. I chose to remain confident that God's plan for me included marriage, even though evidence appeared to the contrary.

An advocate of marriage and believing for my own one day, I still never considered myself a starry-eyed young woman imagining the day I said "I do" would be the most epic moment of my life. I always pictured my most extraordinary day as an amazing comeback of sorts. Oh, what I didn't know . . . or maybe what I did.

The sting of Mitch's rejection triggered crippling tears and led me to throw myself at the feet of Jesus in sheer anguish. I had no idea what to do or what to believe. I held onto hope by a thread. Even though my wilderness wandering had not reached forty years, I was approaching my mid-forties. *Lord, do you know the idea of a family is evaporating?* I pleaded with Him for a way out of this deal. Putting my life on hold until someone else "got it" crumbled whatever remained of my pride.

I struggled with feeling I had returned to an endless holding pattern—circling as the Israelites around Mount Sinai—secretly wondering if I would die in isolation without ever seeing the promised land. I clung to the words of the Spirit, *Wait. And, by the way, it's going to look impossible.* In this purifying desert, the Holy Spirit placed my selfishness, fears, insecurities, and longing for connection in His fiery crucible. The sinful motives of my heart rose to the surface like slag as the flames burned away my familiar.

The Wilderness

My good friend George DeJong taught me much about traveling with the Lord along a difficult path. In his book, *In A Word*, he writes, "Following God into the wilderness will test us and broaden us. Sometimes it will make us want to quit. Yet even amidst its harshness, the wilderness can be a place where we discover some of God's sweetest blessings."[102]

Taking teams to the lands of the Bible with George altered my view of the wilderness forever. What would first appear to be an irritating waste of valuable time (not to mention physically miserable) turned into incredibly powerful moments. We often view navigating a purifying wilderness as a punishment of sorts, or at a minimum, an annoying detour that steers us away from the comfort of our goals and dreams. But there's something about hiking through the rugged terrain, feeling the intense heat, then hearing the Lord's whisper that cultivates a *daring* faith.

In the Hebrew language, two of the more common words translated as wilderness are *midbar* and *jeshimon*. Although also depicted similarly as desert, desolate place, or wasteland, they are different and at times severe.

The dry and barren *midbar* wilderness is not far from fertile ground. Bedouin families still live in the *midbar* and wisely direct their flocks to green pastures. "The word [*midbar*] denotes an area without settled inhabitants and without streams of water but having good pasturage for cattle; a country of wandering tribes, as distinguished from that of a settled people."[103]

The most severe and inhospitable desert is the *jeshimon,* where there is no rain or plant life. "It [*jeshimon*] denotes a greater extent of uncultivated country than other words so rendered. It is the most terrible of all the deserts with which the Israelites were acquainted."[104]

The majority of the Israelites' wanderings occurred in the *jeshimon.*

Excess is no longer important in the *jeshimon.* Whatever fleshly desires are keeping us from intimacy with Jesus, simply burn up in the heat. The biggest challenge we face in a spiritual wilderness is the urge to escape as quickly as possible. But an incomplete work puts us right back there again.

For decades, the Hebrews lived in the harsh and brutal *jeshimon,* but throughout the Text the Lord refers to the *jeshimon* (where they were) as *midbar.* When we obediently follow the Lord into our *jeshimon* wilderness, the hostile surroundings shift. His presence alters the discomfort of our refining process as our *jeshimon* turns into *midbar*—all because He is walking through it with us.

The wilderness is where the Holy Spirit does some of His finest work in us, and in that space His voice is most clear. It's almost as if the Lord predetermined the desert would be the ideal setting for us to experience His presence and to hear Him speak. Which might not be far off. The root word of *midbar,* the mildest of deserts, in Hebrew is *dabar,* which means to speak.[105] I love that the desert is exactly where God intends to talk with us, and that in the wilderness (*midbar*) God speaks (*dabar*). It might be that God says more to us when we are in a wilderness. I don't know. But I do know that the purifying desert better postures us to hear His voice. My problem, however, remains to obey what I hear.

Truth be told, I have been critical of how the Israelites handled their purifying trek through the wilderness. They doubted leadership, feared death, and were quick to complain about the food (or lack of it). Some even wanted to return to the bondage of Egypt. Of course, my disparagement of their behavior comes from knowing the rest of the story. Everything worked out. The Lord supernaturally provided food and water. He parted the sea and fell the walls of Jericho. They should have trusted Him at the outset

Yet my struggle mimics theirs. I falter between belief and unbelief. I yearn for what is familiar and safe and blame others if I don't have it. The wilderness repeatedly is where we face our greatest temptations and absorb our greatest teachings, and it provides neither familiarity nor safety. Moses described the experience this way: "You shall remember the whole way that the Lord your God has led you these forty years in the wilderness, that he might humble you, testing you to know what was in your heart, whether you would keep his commandments or not."[106]

The wilderness humbles me. The wilderness tests me. And in that place, I must decide if I will keep His commandments or not. Gratefully, the Lord didn't listen to my grumbling and pull me out of my wilderness. Instead, He steadied my feet along the path and allowed the refining blaze of the *jeshimon* to incinerate my self-sufficiency. As I fell into the arms of Jesus, my trust in His love grew.

The Veritable Reality

Obediently traversing a wilderness and coming out the other side produces more than a momentary end to our complaints, murmurings, or requests to depose the guy in charge. It prepares us to be trusted with a new reality. The pathway through deepens our confidence and hope in the Lord as He reshapes us into a clearer reflection of Him. This was slowly happening to me, I just didn't know it, and I had no idea the magnitude of the job. It resembles growing up. We rarely notice how much we have changed until Aunt Berta points it out at the family reunion. Change becomes our new reality. And my reality was about to be altered forever.

In the spring of year twelve, Mitch told one of my close friends that God had given him visions for his life that he knew he wasn't walking in. Within four months he married someone else.

If you questioned the legitimacy of my story to this point, I may have just confirmed your doubts. You might be convinced I never heard from the Lord to begin with and now debate whether this book is worth the effort to finish. After all, if God really wanted me to marry Mitch, it should have happened.

Before starting to write, I pondered simplifying the words I heard from the Lord to, *God told me to wait and not date,* and omit the part about Him wanting me to marry Mitch Carver. But that wouldn't be true. And if the book started on a false premise, even with valid principles, it wouldn't have ended well. It's like hitting a golf ball. If you're off a millimeter at impact, you may find yourself in deep trouble. So, despite my initial inclinations, I listened to the Lord and the counsel of a good friend to honestly share my story and the subsequent struggle.

The impact of Mitch's choice shook me for months. My heart felt as though it plummeted from my stomach to my feet. I was numb. When I closed my eyes, I no longer held a vision of what would be; I saw nothing. No sounds, no direction, no new words from the Lord. Honestly, I didn't want to listen. I questioned whether God speaks to us at all . . . ever.

Attacks from the evil one pommeled my mind nonstop. *Why did you waste twelve years of your life? You have become a laughingstock. No one hears from the Lord. Your friends were right to walk away.* With my dreams crushed and hope waning, I had no idea how to move forward.

My discouragement easily fed a spirit of discontent which threatened to overwhelm me. I questioned everything: my faith, my wait, my purpose, my life. Discontent, however, if left unchecked will quickly lead us into a pit of despair where we find ourselves authoring a litany of destructive decisions. We soon become addicted to anything that will take away the pain, whether it's social media, money, people, or substances. And ultimately, we end up choosing to isolate ourselves from those longing to help. Especially the One who loves us most: *Jesus.*

In the barrage of uncertainly, I wanted to run and hide. The anguish at times unbearable. Teetering on the brink of despair, I felt the hands of Jesus reach out and grab hold of my heart refusing to let go. He knew the ache of rejection, betrayal, abandonment, and He knew the power of His presence in my *jeshimon* would lift me out of my shame and restore my brokenness.

The day after Mitch's wedding—my dreams now a pile of ash—God released me from my wait and flooded my soul with an inexplicable calm. It was exactly as the Scripture attests: "And the peace of God, which surpasses all understanding, will guard your hearts and your minds in Christ Jesus."[107] The Lord's overflowing comfort that day guarded my heart and saturated my mind with an engulfing stillness that could only have come from Jesus, the One I had fallen in love with in my *jeshimon.*

From the start of this journey, I kept believing (mostly) that I heard from the Lord. Though at times I misinterpreted a situation and found myself misguided, I could never shake the deep assurance and divine confirmation that repeatedly occurred. I am absolutely certain that for those twelve years, I was exactly *where* God wanted me to be, *when* He wanted me there.

If only that revelation stopped rejection's pain.

The sum of our experiences (good or not so good) develop in us an unwavering trust or a vacillating doubt. Trust flourishes when a friend is present in our sorrow, when what is shared in confidence stays there, or when forgiveness is generously offered. And we feel safe. But doubt intensifies the day our parents separate, we lose our job, or we become the victim of abuse, injustice, or betrayal. The trust we once thought secure no longer exists.

By God's grace I didn't bail on my faith. I may have wanted to bail on men for a while, but I longed to trust the Friend who had stolen my heart. Jesus repeatedly proved Himself faithful over the years. He earned my love and wants to earn yours. He will show up for us and transform our *jeshimon* into *midbar*. I know because He did it for me.

After twelve years of obediently following the Lord by drawing near to Him through my *jeshimon*, my heart began to beat with His and I came to know by personal experience what it means to lean on Jesus with all that I am. It's more than believing water is wet, it's jumping in and getting soaked. It's allowing Jesus to smooth my anxious fears and instill within me His courageous power. In that moment, God *dared* to trust me with the veritable reality. The wait was over and what God desired didn't happen.

This is our reality. Situations occur in our lives and the lives of others that the Lord doesn't want. Never is He caught off guard by what takes place. He knows exactly how it will eventually play out and He can make something amazing out of it all. It's just that He doesn't always want what happens to happen. God didn't want the Israelites to walk away from Him again and again. God didn't want King Saul to turn from his faith, David to commit adultery, or Peter to wield his sword.[108] He didn't want Rebekah to deceive her husband or Tamar to seduce her father-in-law.[109] He didn't celebrate when Moses committed murder, Samson broke his vow, the disciples deserted their Friend, or the rich young ruler rejected Jesus' call.[110]

Our Lord is deeply grieved by murder, sex trafficking, homelessness, pornography, broken marriages, and the self-medication of drugs and alcohol. Don't believe the lie of the evil one that your experience is what the Lord wants for you. Choices are made every day that cause Him sorrow. But regardless of the tragedy, trauma, sin, and rebellion, when we turn back to God and choose to follow, the Lord is faithful to bring healing and restoration to the brokenness that began in the garden.

It was during this time, that a friend shared with me a story of a single woman who had been a missionary to China for years. She desperately desired to partner with a husband to reach people for Jesus Christ. Year after year she pleaded with the Lord to send her a godly man. It never happened. Tearful and discouraged she questioned Him, "Lord, I believe You wanted me to unite with a husband to further Your kingdom here on earth. You gave me that desire and led me to pray for it, and he never came. Did I miss You? Was that not Your will after all? Were my prayers in vain?"

As she quietly listened for the Lord, she heard His tender voice to her spirit, "You are right, I did want you and your husband to serve me. And I did answer your prayers. I told your husband my plan too and stirred his spirit to join you in China. He said no."

It is important you don't hear me say Mitch made a sinful choice. I pray the Lord uses both him and his wife in wonderful ways. I am simply trying to articulate what God yearns for us to understand, experience, or do doesn't always materialize. He desires we have godly marriages, healthy relationships, a passion to grow spiritually, and the fruit of the Spirit evident in our lives. But what happens in life, whether to us or by our choice, isn't always what the Lord desires.

The reality is, we all make choices. Some great, some good, some bad, and some outright devastating. Sin (missing the mark of what the Lord wants for us) is alive in this world and our flesh craves what it believes sin will deliver. But sin is never what God intends for us. He hates sin. Not because we broke a rule; God hates sin because it breaks us. Sin separates us from Him. Sin separates us from others. Sin separates us from ourselves. Sin shatters us and fractures relationships. And the separation that results from sin reaps destruction physically, emotionally, mentally, and spiritually.

The Lord did something about sin when He paid the price for it on the cross, and He wants to do something about the sin that may be currently destroying our lives. He is the only One capable of walking us safely through our *jeshimon*, whether we go on our own, someone forces us there, or the Spirit takes us by the hand and we walk in together. But we must turn to Him, we must be obedient.

Obedience

When I was growing up, Mom (the consummate master kindergarten teacher) posted a chart of daily and weekly responsibilities on our bedroom walls. Every accomplished task, from making our beds to brushing our teeth, resulted in a shiny star placed in the respective square. I loved seeing the brilliant colors line my chart. With four of us kids at varying ages, every chart was different. My little sister may not clean the garage, but she could put her toys away.

Unknowingly I was learning obedience, but I wasn't very good at it. The days I completed only part of my list left gaping holes on my chart that stood out for all to see. A star-filled row, however, gave me a wonderful feeling of satisfaction (resulting more from a sense of accomplishment than joyful obedience). Obedience, whether we are happy to do it or not, is an integral part of the purification process. And it eventually produces peace.

Mom's simple chart trained me how to act regardless of how I felt. It taught my impressionable young self how to acknowledge my emotions but not let them rule my life. Had I succumbed to feelings, I would have spent all my allowance on candy, quit when sprints began at practice, and surely bailed on following God into my *jeshimon*. Choosing to obey clashed with my emotions, but each time I obeyed, each time I willingly placed my feelings into the Refiner's fire, it became easier to do again.

The same, of course, is true of disobedience. If unbridled, repeated disobedience will harden our hearts and the voice of the Spirit will become indistinguishable, and we no longer do what we know is right. We've heard the stories . . . the guy who doesn't believe civil laws pertain to him, the girl who would rather steal than work, or the husband who spends time on internet sites creating relational separation instead of working to develop the real connection he longs for. God doesn't need what we give Him, whether it is our service, time, or finances, if the cost is disobedience.

I remember being told to vacuum my room, take out the trash, and sweep the driveway. I took out the trash and picked up whatever specks I saw on the carpet by my bed. I rationalized away my behavior, because the carpet looked better, and the wind blew the sand off the driveway. Some actions resemble obedience, but partial obedience is still disobedience no matter how it feels or looks.

It is easy to allow emotions to rule our decisions, to avoid the hard conversation, to circumvent relationship, and to rationalize to God and others our partial obedience. It's easy to enter the *jeshimon but* leaving it when trouble dominates only harms us. We become insecure and unstable and end up making choices with unexpected consequences.

Emotions may tell us how we feel, but God never intended emotions to determine how we should act. I love how H. Norman Wright says it:

> What a person feels is one thing. What he chooses to do in response to that feeling is another. The very same emotion can be constructive or destructive. The degree to which our emotions help us or hinder us depends on the degree to which we acknowledge them, understand them, choose to channel them through our thought life, and view them from a balanced, healthy perspective.[111]

When I think about obedience, I am reminded of the Old Testament story of Ruth. (Definitely one of my favorites!) A Moabite widow, Ruth didn't go back to her hometown after mourning the death of her husband but instead chose in faith to follow her mother-in-law to the land of Israel. Shame and reproach cloaked them both. Yet Ruth *dared* to follow the God of her new family, even if it meant she may never marry or have children.

Enter Boaz, the kinsman redeemer, and the rest of the story reads much like a romance novel. Ruth's humility and Boaz's faithfulness are inspiring and unique. Throughout the moving narrative, we see Ruth's obedient character and nobility stand out in a world of mediocrity.

Daring to obediently endure a purification process that appears nonsensical, rather than running to what is familiar, thrusts us into relying on God and not our own abilities. Our obedience ultimately produces in us a deeper love for the Lord and the ability to recognize His faithful presence in the middle of every trial.

Our lives will be transformed by surrender and purified through radical obedience. When we *dare* to follow, as Ruth did, to enter the king's court like Queen Esther, or sit at Jesus' feet as Mary sat,[112] it invigorates our spirit and we begin to see situations differently. But our default is to take after Jacob, whose name changed back and forth from Israel throughout the Text as he continued to struggle *with* God and *against* Him, or Jonah, who ran from God and angrily sat under the shade of a plant.[113] Life-altering change comes when we repeatedly do what's right when we don't feel like it, when others aren't doing it, and when the fruit of our obedience is nowhere to be found.

The Man and the Rock

I have often heard the tale of a time the Lord went to a man and told him He had work for him to do. He showed the man a large rock that lay by the side of the road in front of his cabin.

The Lord asked, "Do you love me?"

"Oh, you know that I love you," the man responded.

"My son, I have placed in front of your home a rock. What I am asking is this: two times a day, simply push against the rock."

The man smiled. "I'll do it, Father, because I love you."

Since the man loved God and wanted to be obedient, he covenanted in his heart that the first thing in the morning, every morning, he would push against the rock. And the last thing at night, before he went to bed, he would push against the rock. His love for God compelled him to push against the rock with all his might, using up so much strength that even over breakfast he barely recovered. And at the end of the day, whatever strength he had left in his arms and legs, he would use it to push against the rock.

This went on day after day, week after week, month after month, year after year. First thing in the morning, pushing against the rock. Last thing at night, pushing against the rock.

One day, the evil one showed up as the man was pushing against the rock.

The evil one asked, "What are you doing?"

The man replied, "God loves me, and I love Him. God asked one thing of me: to push against this rock twice a day. So, every morning and every evening I push against this rock."

The evil one looked at the rock, rubbed his chin, then turned to the man. "But the rock hasn't moved."

The man looked at the rock and sighed. It was true. For years he had pushed against the rock and it hadn't budged. The man became discouraged. So discouraged that, when the sun rose the next morning, the man walked by the rock but didn't push against it. And as the sun set, he walked by the rock once again shaking his head but not pushing against it. This went on for several days.

Then the Lord came to the man and said, "My son, I noticed you stopped pushing against the rock. Why is this?"

The man said, "Father, I have been pushing against this rock every morning, every evening, day after day, week after week, month after month, year after year. And Father, the rock has not moved!"

God sighed. "My son, I never asked you to move the rock. I asked you only to push against it. Look what you've become. Look at your arms, how strong they are. Look at the power in your back and in your legs. You are no longer the same person. I never asked you to move the rock. I only asked you to push against it. It is my job to move the rock."

Sometimes the Lord asks us to push against the rock, and we do, all the while hoping it will move. Our rock may be raising children, remaining faithful, or committing to serve. In a result-oriented culture, expending effort, especially in a *jeshimon*, with no visible outcome tempts us to quit. To bail. But along the way, the Holy Spirit faithfully transforms and refines us as we radically obey. It may occur away from the masses where it is hot, barren, and no one is paying attention. But it is in that place where we clearly hear His voice, that He strengthens us to the point where He will trust us with a new reality.

The presence of the Lord may not always produce the outcome we desire, but in His kingdom, success looks like obedience. So let the Lord take what caused us harm, put it through His fire, and turn it into something incredibly beautiful. For hope arises out of struggle. And as we *dare* to trust Him with our lives, we will discover our obedience in the wilderness has purified our hearts.

Chapter 11

TAKING BACK THE GROUND

The vision I held for twelve years now lay in shambles, engulfing my heart in a whirlwind of disarray. A future with Mitch no longer an option, I plunged into a new reality. I felt confident the Lord held me in His hand and that He remained as close as ever, but the overwhelming sensation of loss still left me feeling alone and unsure of the next step.

Losing is never enjoyable whether you're a player or a coach. And it's especially bad when you endure a crushing defeat (like the 105-47 trouncing by the Brazilian National team, where the player I guarded accounted for 45 of their 105 points). While not uncommon to find myself on the short end of the stick, rare blowouts devastated me. Mitch's choice to marry someone else hit me like a massive failure.

While we can all prepare for a test we see coming, the death of my vision was a blindsiding *jeshimon*. I wanted to trust that the Lord would journey with me through the pain and turn my *jeshimon* into *midbar*. I wanted to believe that if I persisted in obedience, He would create beauty out of the ashes of my life. But I had to *dare* to take back the lost ground and shadow the Lord again.

Unfortunately, my lack of originality and creativity left me at a loss over what to do next. My ability to copy or imitate those who were successful would previously illuminate a path forward. In music,

I imitated artists with similar voice tones, like Amy Grant and Karen Carpenter. And I have even been known to perform a convincing rendition of "We've Only Just Begun." In sports, I worked at imitating gifted athletes: how they controlled the game, how they outsmarted their opponents, how they made their teammates better. But it was all just that, an imitation. I suppose if imitation is a form of flattery, a lot of people should feel pretty good right now.

Attempts to mimic others, however, produce an illusion of control and it also delays God's transformation in us. His design is not that we become a carbon copy of someone else, but rather to get us into the shape of *His* ideal for us. And right then, I found myself in unchartered territory unable to identify anyone traveling a similar path and longing for the Lord to restore the years the locusts had eaten.[114]

For years I believed God designed a perfect plan A for me, and my responsibility was to figure it out and fulfill it to the letter. A rule follower by nature, I naturally walk a narrow road. However, in a propensity to hold sway over at least one area of my life, I developed a contingency plan in case things didn't work out with Mitch. I had answered the question, *If I could date anyone, who would it be?*

I should have embodied more faith in my waiting room and not even considered a plan B, but my flesh won. I created a list during my wait, a dream team, so to say, and the man at the top was a faith-filled, handsome, passionate leader of an influential ministry. He was out of my league, but now that the apparent plan A hadn't materialized, I put *my* plan into action and reached out. A few emails later we connected. When he realized I didn't fall into the stalker category, we met. Our relationship lasted six months. Through it all, however, I came face to face with the realization that the top of *my* list, the best *I* could imagine, *my* ideal man, and *my* quest for love was not God's plan A, B, C, or any other letter. In fact, the man I believed would be the perfect husband for me was not.

I've become increasingly more confident that God doesn't have a plan A for our lives, at least not one that we must follow verbatim. What He desires for you and for me is way more important than the school we attend, the career we embrace, the sport we choose to play, or the person we marry. He longs for relationship. He wants our lives intertwined with His. God's goal is not for us to follow the numbered dots to create a flawless picture. Instead, He would rather we press into sweet intimacy with Him, especially when doing so appears anything but easy.

Choosing to trust in the hidden work of the Lord will at times turn arduous and threaten to draw our mind off course. This was true for me. Being in command of what I thought, what I said, what I saw, and what I chose to do all while trying to come back from definitive failure, proved extremely difficult. The temptation to make decisions based on my feelings countered my desire to grow closer to Jesus. I needed to regain control of my mind.

I'm Thinking

Soon after realizing my perfect man wasn't so perfect, I destroyed the *If I could date anyone, who would it be?* list. While I longed for connection, I found none. *What is wrong with me?* Discouragement repeatedly peppered my thoughts and I fought to manage the mind chatter.

The barrage of wayward mental images reminded me of my introduction to the online game Tetris. For a math lover I found the geometrical shapes addictive. One night after everyone retired, I stayed up and continued to play. (You know, trying to get to level twelve.) Finally, I went to bed. When I closed my eyes, all I saw were steadily cascading tetrominoes that I couldn't make stop. In that moment, I no longer commanded my thoughts.

I never played the game again.

Whether imitating lives of those I admire or trying to determine next steps toward a perceived plan A, I find my greatest battle doesn't involve a game; it occurs in the seven inches between my ears. Left unchecked, I easily succumb to fearful thoughts that flood my head clouding my beliefs. My vivid imagination drives anxiety, creates suspicion, and quickly alters my feelings about the future unless I become an active thinker. While I may not be able to dictate my circumstances, the choice of what *stays* on my mind remains mine.

Deciding to follow the Lord well involves doing our best to control what we think about. Author and trauma specialist, H. Norman Wright comments on the power of our thoughts this way:

Our thoughts influence our character, shape our attitudes, determine our behavior, affect us spiritually, and even influence our immune systems. Our thoughts create emotions that can have lasting physical effects on our bodies. If we dwell on old hurts and wounds, we build a mental habit. That's how the past can dominate the present. Every time we think about the pain from the past, stress—and its toxic effects—surfaces with increasing speed. Each time we think that negative thought, we build a stronger pathway to that negative emotion, and we're more likely to express ourselves in a negative way. Just think of that thought as a cutting tool creating a groove in the brain. Each stroke makes the groove a little deeper, a little more permanent.[115]

Recurring thoughts of humiliating failure propelled me to refocus my mind and stop passively allowing myself to dwell on whatever entered my head. The apostle Paul's directive to "take every thought captive"[116] depicts a fight. And on this battlefield (the one in my head) the evil one endeavored to dominate as much as possible. I needed to counter his attacks.

When I began studying for a career in education, our professors insisted the brain was static. The charge fell on teachers simply to do their best to help students learn to compensate for any learning deficiencies. About the same time, cognitive neuroscientist Dr. Caroline Leaf chose to believe in the malleability and renewability of the brain. Countering the scientific community, her study produced remarkable results on neuroplasticity, the ability of neural networks in the brain to change and grow. Research now shows amazing success in retraining the brain. Studies reveal that 75 to 98 percent of mental, physical, and behavioral illnesses come from our thought life.[117] What we allow to consume our minds will ultimately end up controlling our lives.

Dr. Leaf affirmed what's written in the Text (as if that's necessary), that it is totally possible to take back the ground we have given to the enemy, to "not be conformed to this world, but be transformed by the renewal of your mind."[118] I had allowed the enemy space in my head to breed discouragement and discontent and I aimed to take it back. Making worship a weapon of warfare in the battle for my mind became transformative.

Authentic worship invites us to encounter the Lord and ultimately leaves us in awe of Him. After all, that's the point: to stop staring at ourselves and fix our eyes on Jesus. We can worship the Lord by praising Him for who He is, quoting Scripture, listening to music, or just being still in His presence. Worship is always precipitated by a humble heart, which inevitably draws us closer to His.

As I fought to take my thoughts captive and not allow my plans to usurp God's or my doubts to quash my spirit, I began to memorize longer passages of the Bible. I knew my mindset would determine the direction of my future story, and I knew whatever or whomever I listened to would greatly influence what I believe. So I read the Word out loud to set my mind on things above, not things here on earth.[119] And when my mind started to wander (which, given my situation, was often) I looked for a podcast that targeted my struggle. Depending on the day, it may have been one on bitterness, repentance, or an exposé on the Text. Then I turned up the volume so loud it literally drowned out any negative notions. The living Word of God repeatedly altered my thought trajectory when destructive fears raced through my head.

Maybe you need to reclaim your thoughts and take them captive too. Maybe you feel discouragement setting in at work, at home, or in your marriage and you don't see how it's ever going to improve. When you don't know what to set your mind on, try heeding Paul's advice out of Philippians 4:8-9: "Whatever is true, whatever is honorable, whatever is just, whatever is pure, whatever is lovely, whatever is commendable, if there is any excellence, if there is anything worthy of praise, *think about these things*." And then speak them out loud.

I'm Just Saying

It took work to refocus my mind off my apparent failure. But once my thoughts slowly began to shift off myself, I started to pay attention to what I said, especially about my future. Did my words reflect the truth of the Text or only what I felt? Was my speech expressing faith or tempting me to drift into waves of doubt? When circumstances appeared hopeless, critical thoughts made sounding optimistic a formidable task. It took a conscious effort to speak truth when truth didn't match my feelings or my current situation. I repeatedly needed to remind myself of who the Lord said I am regardless of what happened (or didn't happen) around me.

The evil one hates it when we know who we are in Christ, and he really hates it when we verbalize what we believe. He knows the Text better than we do and he realizes we will become what we think about ourselves. "For as he thinks in his heart, so is he."[120] The evil one doesn't want us to imitate the Lord or learn to "speak of the nonexistent things that [He foretold and promised] as if they [already] existed."[121] But the more we speak truth, the more it settles in our hearts and helps us believe the unbelievable (which I still wanted to do). Turns out, God's Word holds the only truths overflowing with transformational promises. Audibly expressing these confessions on a regular basis infuses me with the power of courage.

Consider these truths about who you are as you say them out loud:

I am praising the Lord with my mouth (Psalm 34:1)

I am kept in safety wherever I go (Psalm 91:11)

I am loved with an everlasting love (Psalm 103:17)

I am the light of the world (Matthew 5:14)

I am taking authority over the enemy (Luke 10:19)

I am clothed with power (Luke 24:49)

I am loved by God (John 3:16)

I am at peace with God (Romans 5:1)

I am dead to sin and alive to God (Romans 6:11)

I am led by the Spirit of God (Romans 8:14)

I am a child of God (Romans 8:16)

I am more than a conqueror (Romans 8:37)

I am transformed by renewing my mind (Romans 12:2)

I am victorious through Jesus Christ (1 Corinthians 15:57)

I am walking by faith and not by sight (2 Corinthians 5:7)

I am a new creation (2 Corinthians 5:17)

I am a minister of reconciliation (2 Corinthians 5:18)

I am taking every thought captive (2 Corinthians 10:5)

I am a child of the promise (Galatians 4:28)

I am saved by grace through faith (Ephesians 2:8)

I am empowered by God (Ephesians 3:20)

I am an imitator of Jesus (Ephesians 5:1)

I am getting all my needs met by Jesus (Philippians 4:19)

I am set free from the power of darkness (Colossians 1:13)

I am forgiven (Colossians 1:14)

I am healed by His stripes (1 Peter 2:24)

I am casting all my cares on Jesus (1 Peter 5:7)

I am daily overcoming the enemy (1 John 4:4)

Speaking the truth of the Text allows the Holy Spirit space to encourage us to believe we are who God says we are. Maybe it's second nature for you to be positive, but for me it is counterintuitive. I struggle to say nice things about myself, which is why I need a list. If I'm not careful, I beat myself up so badly the evil one doesn't have to lift a finger.

"Why, my soul, are you downcast? Why so disturbed within me? Put your hope in God, for I will yet praise him."[122] Here the psalmist deftly expresses their lament and doubt but comes back to the truth. That encourages me. When my heart is heavy and my spirit crushed, I say out loud what I know is true. It might be a confession of who I am in Christ, or a passage of Scripture, or simply repeating the name of Jesus over and over to comfort my soul.

For my words to be consistently life-giving and not life-taking, I must choose to spend time in the right place and with people who also speak truth. Faith-filled individuals have become a means to affect what I think, what I feel, and what I say. Being around those who speak positive words enables me to be clearer reflection of Jesus, to stay healthy, and to be more compassionate.

In the same way, those who regularly spew out destructive comments are people I need to avoid. Negative self-talk robs me of focus, creativity, and the ability to love well. When negative thoughts alter my own feelings and cause my words to become harsh and critical, the Holy Spirit lets me know I am once again the center of my world. Putting myself in a place to regularly hear His truth halts the waves of pity from flooding my soul and my words turn positive again.

I'm Seeing

You're probably not surprised that our thoughts greatly influence our feelings and ultimately what we say. But what we see also impacts our lives in ways that may not yet be fully understood. We are moved by a magnificent picture, a gorgeous sunset, and a smiling baby— and gazing into the eyes of another for any length of time can't help but create a connection. Even so, many undetectable agendas gain entrance into our lives through what we see, and this too will impact our thoughts and feelings, good or bad. But it's easy to ignore what we know and continue to surf internet sites and watch Netflix shows that portray choices in opposition to the Word.

Many believe the lie that watching lifestyles we disagree with won't affect us. However, "a handful of brain-scanning studies show that several regions of the brain are activated during both action execution and observation, and it has been suggested that these areas constitute the human mirror system."[123] In other words, when we repeatedly watch someone do the right thing (or the wrong thing) it begins to create a pathway in the brain that opens the door to subconsciously imitate what we see.

Subliminal messages purposefully disrupt our worldview whether it be through movies, magazines, memes, billboards, or social media, creating indelible pictures in our minds that are difficult to remove.

One of our best defenses is not to allow them in from the start. To turn away from negative images, avoid certain entertainment, and do our best to exit quickly in the check-out lane at the grocery store.

Elite athletes understand the power of the mind and highlight the mental as well as the physical aspect of their performance by pushing out negative influences and making triumph the focal point. The best coaches teach to visualize success and to imagine perfection by encouraging athletes to picture victory, years, months, weeks, days, and even hours before the actual competition. Many skilled musicians and vocalists will practice in front of a mirror to develop confidence for an upcoming gig. What one pictures in their mind changes the way they practice, what they believe, and ultimately how they perform. And what we allow our eyes to see changes us too.

A fellow teacher once told me that when our eyes come across words in a familiar language, our subconscious will automatically read what's written. True or not, I now put in front of my eyes what I want to believe so my mind encounters truth and forms life-giving pathways. I place Scripture on the walls of my home, and currently my kitchen cupboards hold the words, I. Trust. In. You. God., on five colorful, 8-1/2 x 11 pieces of paper. Even when I may not feel it, my mind reads the truth of those words and I change from the inside out. I choose to believe, "If your eye is healthy, your whole body will be full of light."[124]

What we see affects our thoughts and our thoughts transform us. I remain baffled by the story in Genesis of Jacob and Laban. Jacob told his uncle his plans to move from the land and take his wives and children. Laban, while appearing to be generous, said to Jacob that when he decided to leave, he could have all the striped, spotted, or speckled lambs and goats in the flock. Then in the middle of the night, Laban took all the striped, spotted, and speckled animals out of the flocks and sent them to graze far away.[125]

Unfazed by his uncle's antics, Jacob cleverly took sticks of poplar, almond, and plane trees and peeled streaks in them, exposing the white of the sticks. Then he put those sticks in front his flocks. The Text goes on to say that whenever the stronger of the flock were breeding, Jacob placed the sticks in the troughs *before the eyes* of the flock, that they might breed among the sticks. The flocks bred in front of the sticks and brought forth striped, speckled, and spotted lambs.

What?

The Text appears to imply that when the flocks *saw* the streaked sticks and bred in front of them, they gave birth to streaked offspring. Could it be what we see influences us in ways we have yet to grasp? And if that's true, what will we *dare* do as a result?

Do It

Our thoughts precipitate what we do. Even behaviors we may now consider intuitive we once ruminated over. On the flip side, specific actions enable us to think more clearly. Some will debate that we think ourselves into a new way of acting, while others believe we act into a new way of thinking. Both are probably true. For me, certain endeavors do wonders for my mind. Taking a walk, singing, biking, running, or participating in any variety of activities make it much easier to stay positive. You might prefer attending a Zumba class or playing pickleball. Either way, the physical, mental, and emotional benefits help to maintain a constructive mindset.

Another plus to physical activity is the opportunity to be around people while sweating out my stress. It forces me to engage with others and to think about something else. Simultaneously listening to podcasts or music is great too. (I love to multitask!) Controlling what enters my mind and keeping my body strong empowers my spirit when I feel emotionally weak.

If you want to act into a new way of thinking, step in and help someone in need. It may be visiting a widow, taking food to someone ill, writing a note of encouragement, joining a mission's trip, or simply finding an area to serve your community. Reaching out to bring joy to others, diverts attention off our own challenges and begins to build a positive pathway in our mind.

What will you choose to think, say, see, and do? The "devil made me do it" doesn't cut it anymore. Our thoughts, our words, and what we watch will transform the condition of our hearts and lead us to live differently by either drawing us toward or pulling us away from God's ideal. Psalm 1 starts off by saying, "Blessed is the man who walks not in the counsel of the wicked, nor stands in the way of sinners, nor sits in the seat of scoffers; but his delight is in the law of the Lord, and on his law he meditates day and night." The progression is clear. Whom will we choose to walk with, stand next to, or sit and join in conversation? If we decide to walk in the counsel of the wicked, we will end up sitting with the scoffers.

So, in the middle of my doubt and what appeared to be abject defeat, I began to take back the ground I gave to the enemy by *daring* to match what I thought, what I said, what I saw, and what I did with what the Lord wanted for me, trusting He would make my path straight.[126]

I had no idea how the pieces to my life's puzzle were going to fit together or even how many pieces were in the box, but I *dared* to trust that the Lord would one day reveal His plan. Until that time, I endeavor to pray in faith, think in faith, speak in faith, and walk in faith, no matter how my circumstances make me feel.

I. Trust. In. You. God.

Chapter 12

A Personal Plan

I treasured every opportunity to coach, teach, and sing. Fulfilling those roles with excellence, however, made finding time to meet eligible men difficult. So along with millions of others, I went to the internet. Online dating presents its own set of challenges and takes practice to navigate well. Over the course of a few years, I encountered men who posted photos of someone else, some who pretended to be fifteen years younger, and others who were married. The process proved both disheartening and hopeful. I chose to stay positive, and even fell in love with a wonderful man, only to discover our disconnect regarding marriage. Over time my hope began to wane as exhaustion grew with each failed relationship.

Then one day I clicked on Clark's profile. He lived two hours away, shared a love for Jesus, and radiated an infectious smile. My heart skipped a beat. Dad always said I should allow men to make the first move, and most of the time I followed his advice. (Except for my *If I could date anyone list*. And we saw how well that turned out!). So, I waited.

Soon Clark sent an inviting and much welcomed first message. Hearing his story stole my heart. A widower raising teenage triplets captivated me. While a dad and three adolescents might scare some away, the high school teacher in me found the idea irresistible. We exchanged messages over the course of a few weeks and eventually agreed to meet. He first suggested a parking lot, which I quickly nixed, and we settled on a local pizza parlor.

Clark charmed his way through a lovely evening. He possessed an electric passion for life and faith, and a refreshing love for family. His gentle spirit drew me in. Four hours later I knew I'd met a special man. Over the next few months, we got to know each other's families, talked on the phone for hours, and spent weekends making hometown visits. He introduced me to wonderful, faith-filled friends in positions of influence and ministry, and I felt safe.

My heart drew even closer to Clark when I discovered he made clandestine trips to Michigan to sit with Mom for the afternoon or do yard work at my home. My family loved the triplets and Mom adored their dad. So did I. During one of my Christmas women's events, Clark excitedly jumped in to run the product table and champion my passion to share Jesus. The day he showed up at my classroom with flowers, I was smitten. Plans for a future together rapidly fell into place.

As a career high school teacher, it was not lost on me that I met the triplets as they entered their freshmen year. During our time together the Lord revealed delightful individual connections with each one ranging from music to sports. I played basketball and shared a love of math with Ryan, golfed with Ben and reveled in his participation in show choir, and enjoyed shopping and running 5Ks with Grace.

When Clark's family met the McFarland's, Mom was already in the throes of a battle with cancer. He asked for her blessing on our marriage, and she wholeheartedly offered her love and support. Three months after meeting Clark she was gone.

Mom's loss pierced my soul. Her ever-present smile, joyful countenance, positive outlook, and rock-solid faith inspired me like no one else. Being in her presence always lifted my spirit. I yearned to walk through the long-awaited joy of marriage with her, except that was not the plan. The loss of my one remaining parent left me feeling orphaned, and the loving embrace of a new family helped fill the void.

I was thrilled Mom got to know Clark and feel my excitement at becoming a wife and instant mother. Mom gifted me with a clear example of how to serve faithfully, sacrifice completely, and love passionately. Her faith left an amazing legacy on which to build my life. Secretly I prayed for a double anointing of whatever she had to fall on me. As I mourned her absence, I joyfully anticipated our upcoming marriage.

Change Is in the Air

Four months after we met, with help from the kids, Clark surprised me on a dazzling winter night with a gorgeous luminary-lined path that led to a magical marriage proposal. Planning to marry during spring break left us with only three months to pull a wedding together. Once the school year finished, I would move from my home in Michigan to his in Indiana. Blissful pieces of a beautiful ceremony perfectly fell into place. Between worship songs drawing our focus to the One who taught us to love, a nephew walking me down the aisle in his Marine dress blues, handwritten vows, and a unity candle lighting with the triplets, there wasn't a dry eye in the place. My heart overflowed.

After the fairy-tale ceremony, friends and family celebrated at a reception that included two arcade basketball games and a flat screen streaming March Madness. A large contingent of teenagers made the photo booth, music, and our family dance a big hit.

Then came ten incredible days honeymooning in the Costa Rican rainforest!

I never imagined myself at fifty-one marrying for the first time and becoming a mother to boot. Elation and trepidation led a host of new experiences as the career I loved for thirty years ended and my world flipped on its head. My prayer as a teenager for a different life now became a stark reality. Gone were my home and available access to family and friends. I even stepped away from speaking and singing engagements for a year to pour into my new family.[127]

Before long everything familiar disappeared and I found myself living in a log cabin in rural Indiana. I had to adjust to sleeping in a bed with someone else, the sound of people walking down the hallway in the middle of the night, and cooking more than once a week. I also had to acclimate myself to a house full of guns. Avid hunters, my husband and sons only needed to walk out the garage and into the neighboring forest to climb into a tree stand. Soon I tracked deer in camo.

Although my dad grew up in the rural Midwest, the extent of our family firearms included a BB gun. The rifle leaning against my son's bed took some getting used to. One weekend morning, while gazing out the kitchen window, I noticed a coyote crossing the backyard. Clark told me to wake Ben, who bolted out of bed way faster than on school days. Being winter and only in a pair of shorts, Ben ran to the dining room table rifle in hand. He slid into a chair and proceeded to slowly crank open the window and take aim. Then he turned his face toward me and whispered, "This could get loud."

You're kidding, right?

I ran to find Clark who by this time had disappeared outside. I never saw him, but I heard a strange howling noise coming from the shadows near the side of the house. It was Clark attempting to lure in the coyote. Although Ben never ended up with a clear shot, I knew I was not in Kansas anymore. Well, maybe I was in Kansas . . .

Good Versus Best

My personal plan took a rapid turn down an unforeseen path. And through my rose-colored glasses, the road ahead looked wonderful! Not once did I envision ending my career, moving to another state, and raising teenagers, all with a man I knew for less than a year. Then again, rarely will our plan match God's design. Instead, we formulate dreams of what we hope to do or who we'd like to become. And that imagery may be concrete, such as pursuing a specific career or traveling to Europe. Or it may be intangible, such as growing in kindness and faith.

Regardless, no matter our goals, they are just that... ours. We think that our life plan, our normal, our expected reality, and most importantly, our beliefs will make us happy. We never hope for tragedy, suffering, or loss. We never dream of legal trouble, illness, or divorce. And surely God would not orchestrate or allow that to happen to us either. After all, life is good (I'm sure I've seen that on a T-shirt somewhere).

Many presume millennials have cornered the market on entitlement, believing in the claim to perpetual happiness. But they don't hold an exclusive. Adults confidently assume a loving God will always lead to a place of comfort. And when we do the right thing, the right thing will happen to us. In turn, we end up creating a visual representation of what we believe we deserve and not what is real. Just look at the joy-filled, perfectly posed photos we post on social media. Yet no family lives in eternal bliss.

Amid what appears to be a picturesque journey, a sudden change in course may catch us off guard. Even so the Lord is never surprised. Long before our first breath, He envisioned us; ordaining and preparing our days ahead of time.[128] God forges a unique path for each one of us, and His personal plan for me transformed everything familiar.

My only confidence came in knowing that by following the Lord I had landed exactly where He wanted me.

Choosing to adhere to God's personal plan often requires a willingness to give up something good to embrace His best. Still, how do we determine the difference between the two when we can't locate a billboard on the highway or an angelic messenger revealing the next turn?

Consistently opting for God's best necessitates relationship with Him, because on our own we can't figure it out. Only the Lord defines what is good and best, and simply put, His best may not look that way to us. We just can't see as He sees. Yet that doesn't imply an inability for us to follow Him well. By talking with Him, abiding by the guidance in the Text, and listening for His Spirit to speak to ours, God's purpose often becomes clear. And when His plan doesn't appear great at the start or even along the way, continue to hold on.

Jesus demonstrated how to discover God's best personal plan. During His ministry, people pleaded for Him to go to their town and perform miracles (I'd have surely echoed a similar sentiment). Nevertheless, every morning Jesus checked with His Father to discern the plan for that day.[129] Jesus could have chosen to spend His time meeting needs and feeding multitudes, which are really good things, but that's not the reason He came. The Creator, now living among the created, willingly restricted Himself to a physical body, veiling His glory as the One and Only, and chose to act solely on His Father's initiative. He passed on what was beneficial to pursue God's ultimate call—to live, die, be buried, then rise again—all for the forgiveness of our sins. Jesus sought communion with His Father and obeyed what He heard. His daily conversations with God enabled Him to choose the best and stay the course.

Like Jesus, we need to talk with our Father to share our hopes, dreams, and desires, and then surrender to His. If we fail to ask God for direction, we will end up needing to relinquish our plan and recalculate. Wisdom says seek the Lord at the onset, however, that is not intuitive for anyone.

Throughout the Text we see insightful illustrations of those who failed to seek the Lord and choose His best. Sarai, on her own volition, told her husband, Abram, to sleep with their Egyptian servant; Joshua made an ill-advised alliance with people down the street; King Saul chased the anointed David and consulted a witch; and Solomon thought it wise to marry hundreds of women.[130] In the end, the people of Israel suffered because their leaders failed to turn to God in a moment of indecision. They did what was right in their own eyes and paid the price.[131]

Our heavenly Father wants to form us into the vision of His ideal and use our giftedness for His glory. Instead, we see our talents and pursue a path designed for our benefit. We exploit our abilities to get what we want. But choosing to leave God out of the mix creates a tragic ripple effect.

Take Samson. A Nazarite from birth, he ate unclean things, was drawn away by the lust of his eyes, killed hundreds with a jawbone, and allowed his hair to be cut. He broke the Nazarite vow (which prohibited everything I just listed) and used his God-given, supernatural power to destroy. In *Make Your Mark: Getting Right What Samson Got Wrong*, Brad Gray writes, "Imagine the potential of Samson had he used his abilities to capture their attention in a redemptive way, rather than a violent one."[132] When questioned on the source of his incredible strength, what if Samson had pointed the Philistines to the one true God? What if Samson had chosen God's best and used his exceptional talents to give God glory rather than further his own agenda? What might happen if we do?

The Lord desires we *dare* trust Him: to *dare* listen for His Spirit and obey, even if what He asks appears strange. Without a doubt the

Lord led me to leave the comfort of familiarity to step into a new adventure with Clark. And it was a grand invitation to follow Him into the unknown. The Lord's personal plan might take you to a place away from family or friends. He may ask you to do something you don't understand. How will you respond?

Suppose for a moment that the Bible said those with dark hair can't eat pasta (I'd be in big trouble), people who live in Michigan will never marry (yikes!), all electronic devices must be shut down on weekends, or to be healed you need to wash seven times in the Mississippi River. Surely God wouldn't *dare* ask we save ourselves for marriage and remain faithful to our vows. Recognizing the voice of the Spirit isn't enough, we must be willing to *surrender* to His prompting.

But it's risky.

Faithfulness to God's personal plan may cost us everything. Daniel knelt by an open window to pray, and the king had him thrown into a den of lions; Stephen's devotion to Jesus got him stoned to death; and Paul, sent to bring the gospel to the Gentiles, ended up beaten and left for dead.[133] Each, trained by the Spirit, willingly stepped into God's best and walked a path that invoked fear, drew ridicule, and elicited doubt. Regardless of how they appeared, how long they remained faithful, or how they felt, they pursued God's best for them, glorifying Him through their lives, even when faced with death.

Some will argue it's impossible to know what's best. Allow me to push back here. We often become educated far beyond our level of obedience. We know the better choice; we simply don't want to make it. We know we should wait before sending a reactive text, we know we should pray for those who continue to hurt us, we know when the Spirit prompts us to do good.

Now in a new place, I wanted to pursue God's best and not end up traversing a path meant for someone else. I wanted to stick to His plan for me. It didn't take long before an area school approached me to coach and teach (a very tempting proposition) but returning to the gym or the classroom wasn't God's best anymore. While my default regularly fell to glancing at others to determine my next move and chasing after what may be good for them, choosing that path would pull me away from God's best for me. My best now included trusting the Lord to daily show me how to grow to be a godly wife to Clark and a mom to Ben, Ryan, and Grace. I needed to keep my eyes on God's personal plan for me.

The Lord clearly and purposefully led me to Clark, to Indiana, to brand-new relationships. And despite the plethora of massive changes on the horizon, I never questioned the assignment. Marrying a man fervent for his faith in Jesus Christ was cheered on by friends and family and validated by solid believers on both sides of the aisle. Admittedly this current journey felt like the start of a game where players nervously gather at mid-court for tip off, adrenaline pouring through every inch of our bodies, not knowing what the next few minutes would bring but oh so ready to play. Little did I know how well the Lord had prepared me for this new role. The undeniable affirmation from His Spirit kept flooding my heart with peace.

Becoming a welcomed member of another family, especially one that continued to grieve the loss of a wife, mom, daughter-in-law, aunt, and sister-in-law, brought inevitable challenges, yet I remained ready to walk with the Lord and my husband through whatever lay ahead.

Although the Lord prepared me well, my default continued to be to look left and right instead of up. And I soon discovered that spending excessive time observing others (especially online) provoked frustration. Virtual communities make us wonder why we don't feel as happy as others appear. As a result, we fabricate our own reality and use social media sites to produce movies in which we star. We become captivated and diverted by a world of altered truth and struggle to determine what is veritable and what is not.

A bit like a castle in the air.

In our flawed assessment of how we measure up with the cyber world, we inevitably fall short. Wanting my family and friends to graciously accept my feeble attempts at mothering and marriage, I easily succumbed to the internal pressure and resorted to trying to be (or at least looking) like everyone else. The pictures I posted online (especially from our wedding) appeared glorious and somewhat idyllic, though few knew the ongoing loss felt by my husband and kids. The void caused by their loved one's absence didn't vanish just because I entered the family. And pictures, while worth at least a thousand words, fail to tell the entire story. We fool ourselves into thinking if we look good, we are good. And in the tension, we wrestle. Will we *dare* obey the Lord and pursue His best or will we, like lemmings, chase the masses over a cliff?

In this dichotomy we grapple with trying to be something or someone else in our attempt to manufacture a more desirable, or in some cases, a more instantaneous reality. We are driven by what others think or what we think others think or where we think God is leading. Yet rarely does the Lord anoint us and appoint us on the same day.

Before David became king, he faced his biggest battle to date. In his appeal to bring glory to the God of his fathers, he stepped forward to face Goliath. Fearing the worst, the king's advisors persuaded him to first put on Saul's armor.[134] After stumbling under the weight and limited mobility, David had to set it down. Being like King Saul wasn't working for him. He needed to be who God wanted him to be: David, the boy great with a slingshot.

Talent, giftedness, and charm are innately mistaken for God's call leading us to conjure up a vision that may simply further our own ego rather than adhere to His personal plan. I know, I tried writing songs—*not my gift mix*; I tried teaching elementary students—*they are way out of my league*; I tried sewing my own clothes—*what was I thinking*. As my friend George says, "When we don't know what we don't know, we think we know." Oh, what I didn't know! I thought for sure I would coach until they painted my name across the court. Instead, I readily let go of the good in my life to *dare* make room for God's best. Although the Lord's personal plan led me down a new road toward an unidentified destination, I believed He had prepared me for the days ahead.

Preparation

Occasions to choose God's best often appear random and sudden, and they aren't. The Lord secretly prepared them for us, and He has been preparing us for them. We need not despise our days of small beginnings.[135] Moments that seem trivial and insignificant might just transform the course of our lives.

I love watching the Olympics and especially the wonderful vignettes the networks create to highlight how a potential gold medalist with humble beginnings landed in that space. Without exception, each story involves years of preparation and commitment. However, just because athletes and their families make incredible sacrifices, the distinction of making the team or earning a gold medal is never guaranteed. Few athletes are shocked when chosen to represent their country in the Olympic games. Honored? Yes. Surprised? No. They prepared long and hard for that incredible opportunity. Yet many who trained for years still miss the cut because extraordinary commitment to workouts offers no promise of success. And devoid of preparation, athletes—really all of us—will fail to thrive in God's personal plan.

Growing in our relationship with the Lord is like preparing for the Olympics only with greater eternal rewards. Faithfully mining the Word so it seeps into our soul, surrendering in the little things, trusting Him when we can't see, and sacrificing our will for His, year after year and decade after decade, keeps us humble in our success and equipped when dreams are shattered. Those choices give us the ability to obey the Lord even when life flips on its head. And as with the training of many great athletes, businesspeople, or successful artists, intense preparation occurs when no one else is watching. As author Wayne Stiles put it: "God sees our faithfulness in obscurity as preparation for increasing influence."[136] Faithfully pursuing the Lord when days are long, hard, and lonely, prepares us for what is to come.

Whether our preparation leads us to a skill, a university degree, a performance, marriage, or parenthood, we are acutely aware of our focus: why we do what we do. When we obey the Lord, knowing *why* or understanding *what* is not always clear. We can be absolutely certain He is preparing us for something, we just don't know what.

My new marital adventure thrust me into abject dependence on the Lord while blindly racing toward the next bend. The things I thought important (like eating on a schedule or keeping a spotless home) quickly became irrelevant as I endeavored to initiate nurturing relationships. Fortunately, years spent attending marriage conferences, volunteering with young people, and learning to see situations through God's eyes primed me for this moment. Decades of service made it easier to sacrifice my desires and assimilate into a new family.

When we endure through a time of long obedience in the same direction (like a twelve-year wilderness wait), repeatedly abiding by what the Lord asks of us and staying the course when we'd prefer to be rerouted, God smiles. Without embracing faith in the hard times, in the good, and even in the best, it is impossible to please Him. Not just unlikely, impossible.[137] Proving ourselves trustworthy through a time of preparation opens the door for the Lord to use present obstacles to strengthen us to summit future mountains.

The journey we face may involve a significant recalculation (like mine), but rest assured, His personal plan has been distinctively fashioned for each one of us. And if our rerouting takes us into an unpredictable *jeshimon* wilderness on the way, the comfort of knowing we are in the center of God's will empowers us to *dare* continue. In our yielding, we find more than temporal happiness based on circumstances, we experience an inexplicable joy from trusting the character and love of God. As one Old Testament prophet said: "The vision awaits its appointed time; it hastens to the end—it will not lie. If it seems slow, wait for it; it will surely come; it will not delay."[138]

While the vision of marriage I waited for had come in God's timing and transformed daily, my giftings and callings from God remained.[139] He now invited me to love, serve, and reflect Him in a new place with a new family and new friends. Although I held no grid for what lay ahead, I *dared* to venture with Him into the unknown, confident He had prepared me well.

God's Plan for You

What about you? Have you endured a season of preparation that is now beginning to show its mettle?

Preparing for and adhering to God's personal plan for our lives, and not His plan for someone else, gives us the comfort of knowing we are where He wants us to be when He wants us to be there. And should He lead us to an uncomfortable place, the Lord will be faithful to be present with us, saturating us with an abundance of peace and grace along the way.

Thankfully, the Lord's design for everyone (while unique in most aspects) is exactly the same in what really matters: "This is good, and it is pleasing in the sight of God our Savior, *who desires all people to be saved and to come to the knowledge of the truth.*"[140] The substance of the Lord's plan for you and me requires a personal repentance that leads us into a deeper relationship with Him. That's it. He longs for relationship more than our accomplishments or sacrifice. As we humbly acknowledge our need for Jesus Christ and choose to follow Him with all our heart, soul, mind, and strength, we will step into God's best for us.

If you have never opened your heart to a personal relationship with the Lord, do it today. (See the Appendix for more information.) And the indwelling presence of the Holy Spirit will guide you on the most fulfilling journey ever as you step out of what's good into God's best.

Chapter 13

Diamonds in the Rough

"The test results came back. It's cancer."

The doctor paused. Her words hit my stomach like a brick; I could barely breathe. She repeated the findings to be sure I understood. Six months earlier Mom had died of breast cancer and the sorrow from her loss still weighed heavy. Suddenly I approached the threshold of a similar pathway. In my spirit I knew the One who fully loves me held my heart—and this rocked my world.

What will I do now? became instantly replaced by a more pressing thought: *How will I tell my husband?*

Prior to meeting me, Clark had lost his wife following her own ten-year battle with breast cancer. His fifteen-year-old triplets, who just two months earlier had excitedly embraced our marriage, were about to find out their new "mom" received a similar diagnosis. Tears rolled down my face for the ensuing road ahead and for the way it would impact my family.

A month after our wedding I noticed a small lump. Following a mammogram and ultrasound, the doctor recommended a biopsy. My appointments fell during the time I remained in Michigan to finish out the school year. Aware of Clark's first wife's lengthy cancer fight, I held off telling him about my doctor visits until the biopsy, and even then, I downplayed the procedure as somewhat routine inwardly praying it would turn out to be nothing. Sharing the doctor's report with Clark face to face meant waiting for the weekend. The two-hour drive to Indiana felt like five as I nervously ruminated over how to relay my fears while easing his.

Clark sobbed upon hearing the outcome of the biopsy. The fact that I underwent the procedure without him only added to his pain.

Deciding how to best move forward while living in two different states put us both to the test. Clark stepped up masterfully as an advocate with incredible connections. Yet sharing my growing worries with him brought to light his former grief, which proved problematic. I hated that I brought his family into another round of pain and fluctuated between sheltering them from tearful flashbacks and craving emotional support.

We purposefully kept the status of my health close to the vest, sharing it with only a few friends and family members. With the triplets in their first year of high school, Clark and I aimed to protect them from an onslaught of questions by well-meaning outsiders. Plus, I *really* didn't want my identity to become Clark's second wife and the triplets' second mom to have cancer. I wanted our community to get to know me.

I soon finished teaching and gave the commencement address (appropriately titled, "Impossible Is Nothing"), then packed up and moved to Indiana leaving colleagues and students unaware of my emerging health battle.

In lieu of traditional wedding gifts, our friends and family joined together to invest in an incredible two-week trip for the five of us to Egypt, Jordan, and Israel shortly after school let out. Doctors recommended I wait until our return to begin surgery and treatment. I hoped pushing aside my future reality by leaving the country for a while would lift my spirits. But as amazing and adventurous as the trip was, traveling to another continent didn't prevent fearful thoughts from raising their ugly head in the months that followed. *How will I handle treatment? What if I never see the triplets graduate? Why did this have to happen now?*

The future becoming more uncertain by the day, I turned to the Lord just as I had many times before. Prior trials taught me that to live out a faith that *dares*, even while facing a potentially life-threatening prognosis, required that I believe God was good and that His grace would be sufficient regardless of the outcome. As I intentionally focused my gaze on Jesus and not the disease, I felt His presence calm my spirit and provide a ray of hope.

Although the diagnosis was mine, my thoughts lingered more on Clark and how this was affecting him. While it seemed unfair for Clark to consider another trying path alongside his wife, day by day we *dared* to lean on the Lord believing He would guide us well. Clinging to our faith, we pursued a set protocol put in place by gifted and caring physicians.

A plethora of sensations inundated my spirit as I endeavored to make my way down an unfamiliar road. Not having Mom to talk with hit me hardest. She had been my safe place and living apart from all things recognizable added to the tension. As an inherent people pleaser, I made every effort to meet the needs of others yet felt pulled in multiple directions. Clark's family graciously attempted to offer support but wounds from their recent loss remained fresh.

I never envisioned the Lord leading me down such a perilous trail. Yet as I experienced His peace engulf me again, I began to realize how well He prepared me for this journey. Years of leaning on Him as my Savior, Friend, and constant Companion readied me to fight through a medical diagnosis no one wants.

When apprehension and worry hovered like a cloud, the Lord's presence was undeniable. He laughed at my jokes (which I think are hilarious anyway), cried with me when I grieved, and became my shelter in a time of storm. No matter what the day brought, Jesus held my hand, and we walked the road together.

Unexpected circumstances—like sudden alterations in our health—may unsettle us, but they never unsettle the Lord. And each day we choose to pursue His intricate and best plan, He fashions us more in accordance with His vision and reveals more of His heart.

Breathtaking

During our family trip to the Middle East, we visited an old-world shop where before our eyes, they would craft incredible pieces of art from alabaster rock. The owner kindly let me hold one of the natural stones. For its size, the piece was unusually heavy and possessed uneven edges that were rough and sharp. Turning it in the light, a sparkling brilliance hinted at what lay just below the surface. Even its rawness held a distinct elegance.

I watched the craftsman take the rock and carefully chisel away large chunks. He filed smooth the jagged perimeter and with an auger-like tool, began to drill a hole down the middle. Skillfully he dug, shaped, filed, and sanded the stone until a gorgeous vase divulged its exquisite beauty.

It is an impressive gift to picture what others find implausible; to see something invisible to the untrained eye. When I first caught sight of the piece of raw alabaster, I never envisioned anything more than a cool-looking rock. I only saw what I held in my hand. A master artisan imagines something far more glorious and expertly brings out the magnificence concealed beneath the rough exterior.

A guy I know flips buildings for a living. He takes dilapidated structures and transforms them into incredible living or workspaces. Try as I might, when I walked into an old warehouse, I could never picture what he did. I just couldn't get past the rickety walls and the broken windows. It's probably why I am terrible at decorating a home or landscaping a yard. I hold no domestic imagination.

When it comes to people, however, my vision and faith in the inconceivable roars to life. It's as though I see a glimpse of what God does, confident a hidden diamond exists in every soul. My classroom and sport practices held a palpable energy stemming from my vision for the improbable. At times, even with friends, the magnificence I picture makes restraint difficult and (since my greatest strengths are also my most glaring weaknesses) I often share my opinion when uninvited. Now a wife and mom, I see God's potential in my husband and kids and expend significant effort to keep myself in check.

The pitfall of impassioned vision.

While fervent to grow and reveal the unseen treasure in others, I remain oblivious to the diamonds deep below the surface of my own life. So when the Spirit puts me on His wheel and begins to chisel off the pride of needing to be seen, my annoying selfishness, and a forcible impatience, it takes me by surprise. Adjusting to the loss as pieces of activities, responsibilities, or relationships are chipped away, hurts. Yet in the empty space, a fresh normal appears enabling God's beauty to radiate. I longed for His brilliance to shine through as I contended for my health and my marriage.

Rough Edges

During our brief courtship, Clark and I met on weekends and vacation days. He understandably desired more of my time—and I wanted to see more of him too—however, fulfilling my teaching responsibilities and tying a bow on my career made seeing each other during the week nearly impossible. Premarital counsel assured us the resulting tension stemmed from our long-distance relationship and that the frustration would dissipate when I moved to Indiana.

Once we started living together, however, the smallest difference in opinion, choice, or preference fostered the belief I didn't love him or want to be married. I recognized the newness of the marriage experience and my glaring imperfections; still my commitment to love Clark well never waned. The surprising reactions fell outside my limited grid. Growing up with a dad who poured into children as a pastor and educator made me unaccustomed to raised voices unless we were playing outside, and it was dinner time.

Shortly after moving to Indiana, I came across a prayer journal written by Clark's first wife. I quickly discovered the similarities in our experiences as her prayers paralleled mine. I stared at the page in disbelief.

Over the next few years our relationship suffered multiple hits from agonizing revelations. The course of Clark's life prior to meeting me, which holds heartrending trauma and tragedy, is his story to tell and I will refrain from sharing details here. Suffice it to say his past overflowed into our marriage and left me clueless as to how to respond. You would think the shift of no longer working, relocating, battling cancer, and entering the lives of teenagers would create for me the most dissonance—except that was the easy part. The twists and turns of my relationship with Clark shook me to the core.

(Before I go any further, it's important to know that Clark has read this entire book and has given me permission to tell our story. While his name and those of the kids have been changed, I deeply admire his courage and his heart to allow the sharing of our lives to help others better traverse theirs.)

Clark's willingness to meet with counselors gave me hope. Unfortunately, they were unable to comprehend the depth of his pain.

In their defense, Clark was not coming clean. He had mastered the art of hiding his decades-long battles from even his dearest friends. Nevertheless, the Lord persisted in His mission to love Clark, and He chose me to help pull back the curtain.

Three years in, we had worked with ten counselors and attended three weekend intensives. Nothing helped. Even though a successful surgery and cancer treatment left center stage, I continued to feel like a child with no parents in which to confide. I spent my days crying and my nights not sleeping. The fact I recently moved to Indiana made it easy for people to assume the problem lay with me. I found myself reaching out to lifelong friends and mentors to reaffirm truth to my spirit. Years of preparation walking with Jesus in the desert proved their worth and supplied me with the courage and strength to persist. The Lord had faithfully earned my trust during my wilderness wait; I knew He wouldn't let me fall into despair. It just didn't alleviate the massive feeling of failure.

I sensed in Clark a longing to be free from the bondage that held his mind and spirit, yet we struggled to find someone experienced in anything similar. Counsel seemed to default to the obvious . . . we married/remarried late in life, and since I lived alone most of my life (which *obviously* meant I didn't know how to do relationship), we just needed to learn better ways to communicate. Repeatedly counselors gave us an abundance of basic marriage tools none of which addressed the destructive behavior. No one listened to me. And Clark, swimming in his own misery, felt the ache in his soul lift when they assigned me blame.

Not that I was above reproach! I interrupt, react too quickly, and when fearful refrain from saying anything at all. It took way too long for me to realize the futility of providing more information when trying to settle a misunderstanding. Our conflicts had nothing to do with lack of details and everything to do with assumptions and perceptions.

Individual sins wreak havoc in a marriage and lead to marriage problems. And marriage problems, by nature, involve two people. Unfortunately, perception is not reality and making me responsible for the influence of Clark's past on our marriage only applied proverbial paint to a crack in the wall, instead of dealing with the reason the crack was there in the first place. This stymied progress, and church leaders (at a loss as to what to do) encouraged us to pursue individual therapists who never communicated with each other. This didn't help either. I heard I should leave Clark, and he heard I must have deeper issues that hindered me from making him truly happy. It was a mess.

Nonetheless, I refused to end the marriage. A diamond rested deep within Clark that I vowed to help discover for as long as I live. And ending my relationship with Ryan, Ben, and Grace, to me, was unthinkable. Most importantly, God told me not to leave.

I desperately needed the Lord to overcome my inability to fix our marriage. Which meant *daring* to let Him reveal His power through my vulnerability and weaknesses, trusting He would one day bring out the radiant beauty lying deep within both Clark and me. Sharing my marriage challenges with faithful prayer warriors encouraged my spirit and helped to keep me on the right path.

All the while, the Holy Spirit continued to chip away large corners, file rough edges, drill deep into my heart, and sand me down until I more clearly reflected Jesus. I agonized through the process, unaware of His wisdom in shaping seemingly insignificant details into a masterpiece.

Soon after the triplets were born, their mom was diagnosed with cancer and then died a month after they turned twelve. The timing of her decade-long health crisis overlapped with my twelve-year wait. It was no coincidence. While she traversed her own wilderness—her own *jeshimon*—I navigated mine.

No small detail is random to the Master.

God planned my entrance into Clark's family at a specific time, in a specific place, and for His specific purpose. I needed to trust that in the middle of my brokenness He had already charted my path.

Despite a penchant to hope in what I could not see, I struggled to make sense of my new reality. Once thriving relationships now lay in shambles. My inability to be a good friend, a supportive aunt, a caring sister, or to do anything to make my husband happy clouded the image of Jesus I so wanted to display.

Thankfully, the Lord filled me with a supernatural love for Clark, which prevailed over my feelings of failure and loneliness. I longed for the Lord to transform me into the wife He designed me to be— growing in patience, loving generously, believing the best—no matter what it took. Unable to picture what lay ahead, I placed my trust in the Master Artisan and held onto hope that He could.

Radical

The easy answer: get out. The radical choice: swim against the pounding current. Though I wanted to choose the radical way, my present woundedness made it increasingly difficult to rely on what I believed to be true. *Will I risk following the Lord into the turmoil? What if the anguish never ends? Am I standing in faith just to delay the inevitable?* The questions sounded all too familiar. Listening to and obeying the Lord, while still the best choice, offers no assurance life will pan out the way we think it should.

We see it demonstrated in the life of the apostle Paul, who, on the road to Damascus to persecute followers of Jesus, passionately defended the God he knew and in a flashing moment, his world flipped right-side-up. His encounter with Jesus drastically opposed what he understood to be true and upended his assumed reality. He then chose to set himself apart for a season to relearn the Text and come to know Jesus personally. This radical decision revolutionized the world. Be that as it may, radical obedience, like that of Paul or what you might be facing right now, is grueling and rarely celebrated. Often it is ostracized. In our quest for understanding, we try to make sense of a situation so we can better predict a logical outcome. Stepping out to do the unconventional takes radical faith.

Our experience with the living Christ may not be as dramatic as Paul's, yet His voice to our spirit is just as real. He may be speaking as we busily work, or scroll through our phone, or chase kids, or fight for our marriage, or care for aging parents, or do church, or, or, or . . . And unless we quiet ourselves, it will be difficult for His voice to break through. Even experiencing a divine encounter with Jesus offers no guarantee we will follow the Lord and discover the veiled diamonds. That choice remains ours.

Let's imagine for a moment that God first told Jenaz to build the ark, or a guy named Zadok to go fight Goliath, or sent the angel Gabriel to a girl named Haniah? And instead of responding, "May it be to me as you have said," they each replied, "I'm not interested. I am good here, thanks anyway." Their choice thereby opening the door for the Lord to reveal His glory to Noah, David, and Mary. Will we be so bold as to say, "I'm in," or will we tell the Lord to try someone else?

Although the Lord doesn't show us the end from the beginning, I want to pay attention to my inner witness; to do the right thing regarding my marriage even when others scoff. One coaching colleague made shirts for his football team that said, "Work hard. Play hard. Do the right thing." And parents became angry a coach would *dare* suggest there is a right thing.

We must be prepared to hear voices that counter what we know God desires for us and to decide ahead of time how we will respond. Waiting until pressure builds and destructive situations overtake us is not the time to ponder who we want to follow. *Daring* to make step-by-step, radical, right choices to chase after Jesus before it gets hard, allows Him to shape us into something beautiful and infuse us with the power of courage right when we need it most.

The Lord knows within each one of us lies a precious diamond in the rough because He put it there. And He wants to partner with us to further His plan of restoration. Certainly, He can refashion our lives and His creation apart from our help, yet that isn't how He designed His kingdom. He is about relationship. Relationship with Him, relationship with others, relationship with ourselves. I knew He placed a striking treasure within both Clark and me that a growing relationship with the Lord would eventually reveal.

As we *dare* listen to the radical voice of His Spirit and follow, as sure as He is God and we are His, we will turn out exactly as the Master Artisan envisioned. Especially when our path is exceedingly more complicated than we ever imagined. For it's more about the One you travel with than the toil of the terrain.

Are you willing to place your trust in the Lord and lean on Him when what you see up ahead scares you? Will you renew your mind with truths of the Text? Will you speak words of faith? Will you choose to listen to voices that encourage your spirit? By clinging to Jesus again and again—relying on Him when you can find no logical reason to do so—your relationship with Him flourishes, illuminating the marvelous treasure hidden deep within your soul.

Face the Trial

Let's be honest, our first preference isn't to encounter difficulty. We don't intend to wait until past middle age before marrying, receive a cancer diagnosis once we do, and then become a recipient of destructive choices. I don't know about you, but it's not my daily habit to recite the prayer of David that says, "Search me, O God, and know my heart; test me and know my anxious thoughts. See if there is any offensive way in me, and lead me in the way everlasting."[141] Asking God to search my heart and test me is just inviting Him to do a work in me and that doesn't sound comfortable.

Opening the door for the Lord to unveil the brilliance underneath our rough outer shell inevitably leads to pressure, a refinement of sorts. I could feel the heat and the force of His chisel as He eliminated my reliance on others and chipped away at my selfishness. Refusing to contend for the diamond would relegate me to the sidelines and Clark and I would never experience victory. You know what I mean. Your neighbor is rude, your employer unreasonable, and your spouse not at all what you expected. Yet you push past the intense discomfort because you know it's where the Lord wants you. You *dare* to believe that by choosing to do the right thing when you'd much rather bail, a dazzling beauty will one day break through.

Maybe it's why Paul says to the Philippians, "It has been granted to you that for the sake of Christ you should not only believe in him but also suffer for his sake."[142] What did Paul mean, it has been *granted* to us to suffer? When I look up the meaning of the Greek word for granted, *charizomai*, it says to do something pleasant or agreeable for someone, to do them a favor.[143] It's as though suffering provides access to an unexpected gift. That is not my view of suffering, yet it might be exactly what suffering does. Trusting through trial allows the Spirit's masterful and gracious work in our lives to emerge.

Troubles and disappointments are commonplace. *Daring* to face them graciously is not. We see how quickly people unleash harmful words and ghost those they call friends and family members. Instead of holding a live conversation, we hide behind texts and emails and post caustic comments on various media outlets. If we want to stand well during hardship, we need to take the focus off ourselves and fix our eyes on Jesus. And then we will discover that amid our struggle and the temptation to quit, the Lord God will provide a way through *and* the ability to endure.[144] But will we *dare* live as though we believe that to be true?

Be Courageous

When walking through a fiery trial, I don't always handle it well and would rather end the discomfort. Yet I can't expect the Lord to create something beautiful in my life without it. So on a good day, I pray for the ability and the courage to endure and praise God, not for the fire, but for who He is and the purifying work He promises to do in me. To thank Him for my treasured friends in Indiana; to thank Him for my precious young family; to thank Him for refining my heart as He draws me to His; to thank Him for the power to believe He will be glorified in my marriage. To say along with Paul, I will boast in my weakness so that more of God's power will come upon me.[145]

When we are weak (a daily occurrence for me), we must look for the power of the Lord to strengthen us. For our God promises to supply all we need.[146] All we need when we are lonely, all we need when our heart aches, all we need when the world no longer makes sense, all we need when tragedy and trauma become the norm and we no longer know which way is up.

Will we *dare* to be different; to recognize, acknowledge, embrace, and arm ourselves with the authority granted us by Jesus over *all* the power of the enemy?[147] Sometimes we head into a spiritual battle with no more than a cross around our neck, content to hide behind the shield of faith hoping we won't get hit, yet wondering why we aren't winning the fight. Take up the sword of the Spirit (the Word of God) and swing it! Go on the offensive. Courageously confront the enemy head on. It's not hearing the Word that changes our lives; it's the power of the Holy Spirit at work as we faithfully walk out the Text that changes our lives. I pray the eyes of our hearts would be enlightened in order that we may know and use His hope, riches, and power that operate in and through us who believe.[148]

We are not in this battle alone; we are not unarmed. And we need to *dare* act that way. *Dare* to believe the Lord will empower us to do more than just survive difficulty but be victorious. If we believe we have authority over the evil one (the one who would destroy us yesterday if God let him), our words will counter his attacks. As we speak God's truth and stand in faith, His power is released right in the middle of our trial.

In what appeared to be a collapse of my most beloved earthly relationship, I chose to hold onto the truth of the Word, to speak life and hope into my marriage and my husband, trusting the Lord to move in His timing and in His ways. For the greater the opposition, the greater the victory will be.

Let's *dare* to walk toward healing, *dare* to face our addiction, *dare* to swim against the current of mediocrity. Because "in all these things we are more than conquerors through Him who loved us."[149] And one day, we will discover He created in us a clean heart and made our spirit strong again.[150] And the diamond within us will bedazzle us all. For as Jesus reminds us, "What is impossible with man is possible with God."[151]

Chapter 14

HEART FAILURE

The myth of guaranteed happiness comes as a shock to many a believer. Unexpected detours drive us to plead for divine intervention while blaming God for what feels like a misdirect. My lingering marital obstacles sent me stumbling down an agonizing road of rejection feeling abandoned and vastly misunderstood. For decades I sought to follow the Lord well yet current circumstances neither looked nor felt familiar.

Like you, my soul craves to be known and loved by both our Creator and by those I hold dear. Sadly, our culture no longer encourages us to gather with those around us but instead persuades us to stay inside and link to virtual friends. The uncommon knack of relating well to others has even led elementary teachers to create classroom friend groups that teach how to ask questions, how to be kind, and what it means to be a good ally.

By the time I was a teenager, I held a vague idea of how the Lord directed my life and how relationships meshed with His plan. My self-absorbed world left me unskilled at relating on a deeper level. The fact we moved seven times before I reached high school played a part. With every relocation I attempted to stay in contact with former classmates and neighbors until sooner or later they stopped returning my calls. It took years to learn to engage others well and not dominate a conversation, and equally as long to realize the delight of giving of myself far outlasts the delight of receiving.

I soon discovered that preserving relationships over many years takes significant effort. Truth be told, some people are only in our lives for a season. We invest our hearts, then one moves away, marries, finds other friends, or just doesn't like you anymore. And it stings no matter how old you are.

I sensed that sting during my wait for Mitch as friends withdrew—convinced that God doesn't lead us into difficulty, therefore, I must have missed Him. Fighting to save my marriage with Clark garnered a similar response as others stepped away unsure of what to do, what to say, and certain I should just leave. I found it hard not to take offense and equally challenging to know how to do wife and mom while balancing whatever relationships remained. I felt alone in another wilderness, rejected, and losing heart.

In my previous twelve-year journey, I endured what felt like an all-consuming desert and collapsed into the arms of Jesus. Now heartbroken over a failing marriage, the Lord pulled me in close again. I ached for approval and love, especially from my husband, and Jesus kept telling me He would be enough. Tearfully I repeated out loud the words of Isaiah 41:10, "Fear not, for I am with you; be not dismayed, for I am your God; I will strengthen you, I will help you, I will uphold you with my righteous right hand."

Connected Where It Counts

When we encounter problems, marital or otherwise, it's normal to seek out emotional support: the hands and feet of Jesus here on earth. I cherish the precious few who faithfully stand the test of time, through death, trial, and loss . . . waiting with me . . . crying when I cry . . . praying for my heart . . . and most of all, challenging me to trust

God no matter how it feels or what it looks like. Just as Aaron and Hur sat Moses on a rock and propped up his arms,[152] true friends point me to Jesus (my Rock) and lift my spirit when strength wanes.

However, it is possible to lean too much on people. If we rely on others to shield our hearts from discouragement and despair in the middle of a crumbling reality (which doesn't work anyway) it prevents us from turning to Jesus. Only by choosing to lean our entire personality on the Lord when facing inevitable trials—*daring* to seek connection with Jesus Christ—will we experience His presence and discover the power of courage to stay the course when we'd rather bail.

In his insightful book, *Practicing the Presence of God*, Brother Lawrence described how he experienced a deeper relationship with God as he endeavored, as much as humanly possible, to be in constant communion with the Lord. Needing to hear from the Lord, I went to my prayer journal as I had many times before. I dialogued with Him and listened for His download to my heart.

I didn't hear what I wanted to hear: that the Lord would fix things and my marriage would soon be miraculously restored. Rather He told me not to take offense, to believe the best, to respond with kindness, and to keep standing in faith. He reminded me to place relationships on His hook and take them off mine; to stop usurping the Holy Spirit's job by trying to change anyone else but me.

I am no longer surprised that when I seek the Lord with all my heart, I find Him.[153] For God, through His Spirit, clearly impressed His words upon the minds and hearts of believers and non-believers all throughout the Text and will continue to do so today if we *dare* in faith that He will and pause long enough to listen. By chasing after Jesus, we remain connected where it counts and shielded from total heart failure.

What Now?

My relationship with the Lord became a lifeline in a time of turmoil. I started to envision healing, to break through fear, and I *dared* to step forward in faith even though I constantly battled the thought I missed God's plan by marrying my husband. But the Lord never let me wallow in that pit of doubt for long. He always brought me back to, *You didn't miss Me. I led you exactly to this place. I have prepared you well.* Although my situation persisted, He spoke tenderly to me in my wilderness and made my *jeshimon* feel like *midbar*.

Clark's willingness to admit his struggle made me believe the worst was over, until new revelations surfaced. I was gutted. I joined multiple support groups to salvage my heart and my marriage. If not for the restraint of the Holy Spirit, I surely would have run from the promise, *'Til death do us part.*

Then came more damaging choices and another confession.

Good or bad, I trust what people say, so I no longer knew what to believe. Our marriage fell into a tailspin and led us to a new weekend intensive. We encountered a wonderful counselor and were moving forward again. Two weeks later Clark left town for work and when he returned, I learned our marriage vows had been broken.

I went to stay with friends for a couple of days. Clark and I opted to live apart as we sifted through the rubble. In my solitude and loneliness, I collapsed into the embrace of the One who really loved me, because I was now convinced my husband never did.

My barely recognizable existence exacerbated my failing heart. With no recipe for what steps to take, I fell back on what I knew about the Lord, what I believed in the Text to be true, and I tried to do the next right thing. Yet some mornings I never got out of bed.

On good days I tried to maintain a semblance of structure: helping those in my neighborhood, serving at church, working out, attending life-giving conferences, and spending time with believers who challenged me to stay faithful when I wanted to run or scream or at times break something. (Yep, found a place where I could do that!) Thankfully, the music and speaking ministry the Lord led me to decades before meeting Clark, kept doors open for me to serve in a variety of capacities even in the middle of my pain.[154] Getting my eyes off myself helped my heart to heal.

I knew that to take my thoughts captive, I needed to stop thinking about what I was thinking about (which is totally possible) and refuse to dwell on how people fail me or my fear of the future. Instead, I could choose to believe what the Word says is true. But fear of tomorrow is paralyzing. I remember the night before recording my first album in Nashville, calling my mom in a panic. I had lost my voice. We were scheduled to lay down vocal tracks in the studio the next morning, and I could barely speak. Mom calmly asked, "Are you recording now?"

"No," I replied.

"Then you don't need your voice right now. Tomorrow in the studio, you'll have it." And I did.

I don't want to lose today by fearing tomorrow, so to renew my mind I listened to podcasts on marriage, participated in webinars, served on music teams, coached at sport camps, led small group Bible studies, read books that helped me stand in faith, and eliminated negative thoughts as best I could. But this time, I was treading in water way over my head.

Go Into the Deep

The Gospel of Luke describes a scene by the Sea of Galilee where people pressed in so close to hear Jesus that He hopped into Peter's boat

181

and had him put out from shore. From there He taught the increasingly large crowds. When He finished, Jesus told Simon Peter to take his boat out to the *deep* water and let down the nets. Peter hesitated as he had spent the previous night on the water and caught nothing but eventually, he acquiesced.[155]

Immediately the nets filled with fish. The weight of the catch threatened to sink the boat until Peter's buddies brought over another to help land the haul. When James, John, Andrew, and Peter finally got the fish to shore, they were so amazed at what occurred, they immediately left their nets (and all their fish) to follow Jesus.

You may remember the story of Jesus walking on water, mentioned briefly in an earlier chapter. After a long day of teaching and miracles, Jesus sent the disciples (who must have been living in constant wonder) in a boat to the other side of the sea. By the middle of the night, the disciples were in the *deep* water far from land. You can imagine their terror when they caught sight of Jesus as He approached on the surging waves.[156]

Despite intimidating fear, Peter boldly asked the Lord if he could walk to Him on the water, and Jesus said come. I find it telling that Jesus didn't first calm the waves but simply invited Peter to step out into the middle of them. As Peter drew closer to Jesus, the journey became increasingly difficult (are you getting this?). Ultimately, when Peter came within an arm's length of Jesus—where the water was *deep*—fear weakened his resolve and he started to sink. Peter cried for help. Instantly Jesus reached out His hand and rescued him.

When the Lord takes us to another level, it happens in the *deep* end of the pool.

Difficulty does not insinuate we have in any way missed God. The *deep* is where we should expect storms and adversity—and it's where His presence becomes more real. Abram followed the Lord to a new land, and he immediately encountered famine. And he was right where God wanted him.[157] The Spirit led the apostle Paul to preach the gospel to Asia Minor and soon after he arrived, he met persecution. And he, too, landed exactly where he was supposed to be.[158]

The presence of struggle, trial, or heartache tempts us to take our eyes off the Lord and, out of fear, pursue an easier path. Sadly, our perceived route of least resistance never leads where we expect and before we know it, we find ourselves alone, in *deep* water, desperately reaching for Jesus.

Jesus invites us to come; to walk with Him where it's *deep*. But *daring* to trust the Savior in the abyss is risky. Until one day we realize that although the water is way over our heads, it is still beneath His feet. For in the *deep*, miracles happen, and great catches are made. We need only to *dare* get out of the boat, to intentionally interact with uncertainty and walk alongside Jesus.

With the Shepherd

During one of my first trips to the country of Jordan, where Bedouin tents and first-century traditions remain, our study group unexpectedly encountered a shepherd leading his flock of sheep and goats. We quickly hopped off the bus, and from our hillside vantage point, watched the shepherd traverse a steep wilderness mountainside looking for food. Eventually he took a seat on a rock and let his animals munch on sparse clumps of brown grass. A young goat, meandering on its own behind the others, ended up stuck on a small precipice. Eight feet above the rest of the flock, he started to cry. Where we sat, a few hundred yards away, we saw the plight and heard the wavering call for help.

The shepherd glanced back at the tiny goat but remained seated on the rock. Soon, other sheep and goats gathered below the kid and commenced their own bleating. They may have been giving direction or trying to get the shepherd's attention, hard to know. But between the trapped young goat and the *baas* of older ones, they created quite a chorus. As the little guy continued to bleat, we wondered why the shepherd, aware of the predicament, didn't go back to help.

After observing the scene for nearly fifteen minutes, we started to question the shepherd's competence. He obviously heard the cries but did nothing. Then ever so slowly the small goat began to inch his way closer and closer to the edge. Suddenly he vaulted off the cliff, stumbling and rolling as he hit the ground. Springing quickly to his feet, he scampered over to the shepherd and nestled in safely by his side.

Like the young goat, we're easily distracted by the next tuft of grass or the thrill of adventure and before we know it, the fold is no longer in sight. Chasing after what feels good draws us away from the safety and care of our Shepherd. But whether we meander away from the path like sheep or a kid goat—fearful or out on a ledge—Jesus hears our cry and provides hope in the simple comfort of His presence.

Jesus never deserts those who inadvertently wander off, have no idea they are lost, or consciously choose to walk away. Like a shepherd relentlessly searching for his one lost sheep, the Lord stays present even when we stray off course. For it is in His presence that He will begin to restore our brokenness. And amid our disappointment, He will prove Himself trustworthy again and again.

I held onto hope that God's vision for marriage would one day be reflected in ours. And I *dared* to believe the Lord wouldn't leave Clark and me to fend for ourselves. That He would pursue us like the woman trying to find her lost coin, scouring every inch of the house to find what had become unknowingly lost, indistinguishable from the surroundings.[159] We identify with that coin and often blend into the woodwork with no idea how far we rolled away from the One who deeply desires relationship.

Our heavenly Father knows when distractions alter our focus, when we get caught in a crevice, or when we decide to purposefully reject Him. And He allows it to happen. He gives us the freedom to follow Him or not; for love is not real if it is not a choice. The day we finally understand the gaping hole in our heart (the one we try filling with people, money, or position) can only be filled by Jesus, we head home to discover, like a father waiting for the return of his lost son, that He is running toward us with open arms. Always.

Whether we carelessly drift off the path, become assimilated into an unknowing culture, or return from a chosen life of disobedience, the moment we are noticed by the Shepherd, the Woman, or the Father, it triggers an amazing celebration. The one who was lost is found.

Now vastly disoriented in my marriage relationship, I prayed we would soon be found.

Take Heart

People willing to step into our chaos deeply loved our family. But until decisions could be made to rebuild trust and create a safe environment, we lived apart. Clark stayed in our house, and I moved into our cottage. Nothing about the separation was easy. Now more than an hour from my family, my church, and my home, I felt uprooted again. Everything became harder for me: maintaining relationships, taking care of another place, finding a new community, and driving lengthy distances to get anywhere. Choosing to fight for marriage (or any other relationship) doesn't guarantee restoration or eliminate angst, neither does *daring* to do the right thing by standing in faith in the presence of apprehension and improbability. I had to trust this was not my battle to win, it was simply my glory to reflect Jesus just by the stand.

Regrettably, those counseling us, though passionate about restoration, had difficulty recognizing that what we faced required more
than a bandage. Counselor Leslie Vernick explains the conventional
default, "We've misdiagnosed a marriage that has terminal cancer and
treated it as if it were only suffering from a common cold."[160]

Contrary to counsel, I held to the belief that Clark's responses were
not calculated. I couldn't acknowledge (and maybe just wouldn't accept)
that this man who possessed such a gentle and compassionate spirit
would deliberately inflict harm. While one therapist said Clark was
purposefully trying to hurt me, I couldn't go there. Yes, his actions tore
me apart, but I chose to believe that wasn't his intent. The depth of his
trauma created strongholds that needed to be broken and tools to walk
it out utilized. As I searched for answers, the Lord brought along a godly
couple familiar with Clark's experience.

Hope grew.

Under guidance of a newly formed care team, I tried my best to
follow their suggestions thinking we had to be moving in the right
direction. Then Clark suddenly said it was over. He found it too difficult to walk through the pain that healing required and simply chose
to avoid it and me altogether.

I was devastated.

I ran to Jesus and sobbed on His lap. A few godly men talked Clark
off the ledge, but he never returned to those willing to help navigate
through the debris. We met individually with our care team and
shuffled counselors again. I felt alone and far from anyone who loved
me. My spirit couldn't take much more. Staying the course wearied
my heart in ways my cancer diagnosis never did.

To refocus my mind on what I could control and release that which
I couldn't, I joined a two-week study trip to Turkey. I returned only to
face questions from church leaders over whether I should be allowed

to continue serving as a Bible teacher and worship leader since Clark and I remained separated. My mind now spun from both jet lag and another rejection. I went off grid for days.

In defense of those who questioned my involvement, they didn't fully comprehend the situation. After a conversation (which probably should have happened on the front end), they reversed their stance and endorsed my participation. Unfortunately, damage to my heart left me licking wounds. My empathy grew for those quickly judged and easily misunderstood, aware that though the Holy Spirit heals our heart, painful memories still elicit tears.

Loss hits me hard. Whether it be the death of family members, the death of a job, the death of a vision, the death of a friendship, or what now appeared to be the death of my marriage. And nothing brings more chaos to life than death. I felt powerless. Although I've never experienced physical heart failure, the rise and fall of both hope and despair were excruciating. You might know the feeling.

In the Gospel of Matthew, friends brought to Jesus a man powerless and desperate for help. Jesus' first words to the paralytic were not to pick up his bed and go home. They were, "*Take heart*, my son; your sins are forgiven." A woman hemorrhaging for twelve years touched the hem of Jesus' garment and was healed. And Jesus turned to her and said, "*Take heart*, daughter; your faith has made you well." As the disciples labored to get their boat to land, Jesus appeared walking on the water. They freaked out until He spoke to them, saying, "*Take heart*; it is I. Do not be afraid."[161]

Jesus encourages each of us today with His timeless words in John 16:33: "I have said these things to you, that in me you may have peace. In the world you will have tribulation. But *take heart*; I have overcome the world."

Take heart—and let Jesus speak into your situation.

Take heart—the Lord is who He says He is.

Take heart—the Lord will do what He says He will do.

Take heart—though loved ones turn from the Lord.

Take heart—when the medical prognosis isn't good.

Take heart—as you stand in faith.

Take heart—in loss and in death.

Take heart—as you step out to follow the Lord.

Take heart—Jesus didn't say He will one day overcome the world. He said He already did.

As much as I exhort faith to believe for the impossible, I know not every story resolves the way we want. Yes, the Lord is more than capable of making something good out of every situation, especially for those who love Him, but the outcome may not be what He desired or what we envision.[162]

Still, I choose to hold on, trusting the Lord to mend my failing heart. And in my weak and weary attempts at praise, I rest in His presence, confident He has not stopped working in me. Many days I pray for more strength, and He ends up *being* my strength. Nevertheless, I *dare* to picture an epic party this side of heaven. But if this is not my end story, my heart rests on the One who will be with me for every step.

Take heart.

Chapter 15

Believe the Unbelievable

A year prior to the disclosure that led to our marriage separation, a friend inspired me to sign up for the Chicago Marathon. Although not a skilled distance runner (which is putting it mildly) I nervously accepted the challenge. After promising my chiropractor this would be a one-and-done event, he gave me the green light and I commenced a ten-month-long training regimen. I wanted to give the race my best shot, but the process was intense. At times I barely survived the long runs and wondered how I would ever handle 26.2 miles. Daily I encountered what people call the lizard brain—that primordial part of my mind telling me to quit.

Training for and running a marathon turned into the most strenuous physical challenge I ever pursued. A week before race day, after nearly a year of preparation, I learned of my husband's betrayal. For days I considered pulling out. And then I recalled the years I spent motivating young athletes to face looming obstacles and not avoid them. So, I chose to *dare* confront that which now felt insurmountable. Though I ran alongside tens of thousands of others (more afore than behind), with each mile I contended more and more with a profound sense of loneliness. Two sweet friends showed up in Chicago to cheer me on as the race became symbolic of the fortitude required to stand in faith for Clark and our relationship. I handled most of the course well but cried my way through the final few miles as I sensed an overwhelming heaviness over what was to come.

I want to believe the unbelievable, that the start of a miraculous restoration lies around the next bend, yet my flesh fights a lingering uphill battle. At the time of this writing, our separation is approaching five years, causing me to daily wrestle with what I know to be true and what I see. Will I remain faithful, or will the voice of the lizard prevail? Some days I ache for the simplicity of a backyard tree fort where imagination rules and dreams become reality; for hope to no longer disappoint and for love to win. But now, more than ever before, I find I crave more of Jesus.

When the Lord imparts His vision to believers, we may try to ignore it or be placated by something inferior but the Spirit of God alive in our hearts will never let us be satisfied in any other place. Surrendering to the Lord our desired destination—willing instead to arrive at His—produces a thirst for the power of His presence. And as we continue to allow *daring* faith in the Lord to become established in our souls, the Spirit emboldens us with the courage to persevere even when surrounding circumstances look less than favorable.

Dead or Alive?

During Babylonian captivity, the word of the Lord came to Ezekiel, and he prophesied to the Israelites in exile. Ezekiel wrote that the hand of the Lord brought him to the middle of a valley full of dry bones. There, the Lord asked, "Can these bones live?"[163] The Lord wanted to know or for Ezekiel to recognize, whether he *dared* to consider what his eyes couldn't see and what was not yet real. Could what's dead come back to life?

The Spirit of the Lord graciously grants me enough courage to envision that my marriage, which appears to be over, will one day breathe again. I want to be certain impossible is nothing when holding onto Jesus, yet my own naiveté may be driving me to reject imminent failure. Is it possible to *dare* so greatly that reality is pushed out the door? Clark has not legally terminated our marriage, which creates for me a cloud the size of a man's hand.[164] I believe Clark wants to be a man after God's heart, however, he has yet to choose to walk a path toward rebuilding broken trust or desire to create a safe place for me— so we remain separated. As I lament to the Lord and listen for His voice, He speaks clearly into my impatience, anger, and brokenness.

Continue to do good. I will sustain you with perfect peace. Place your heart in My hands.

Succumbing to the frustration of the loss of family and a lengthy timetable veils my view of Christ and does nothing to alter the current situation. It gives rise only to discouraging thoughts and harmful emotions enticing me to say or do something I regret. I hate how the evil one attempts to destroy what the Lord designed to be a beautiful reflection of Him by distorting and blurring truth.

At times when facing the destructiveness of deceit, addiction, abuse, infidelity, betrayal, or injustice, sorrow and anger are reasonable responses, maybe even justified. But when we decide in these difficult seasons to express our grief to the One who experienced the same, that choice symbolizes our trust both to Him and to us. For it is in believing God is sovereign that we do grieve, we do lament. And lamenting is part of the healing process. It is a prayer made in pain that leads to even greater trust in the Lord. Lamenting is being honest enough to mourn the loss of something precious even as we return to His embrace. It's not just desperate weeping that endures for a night (or two, or three, or ten), it's an expectation that joy will come one of these mornings.

In shifting the focus off us and onto deepening our relationship with Jesus we experience supernatural courage, a knowing, that as we cling to, rely on, and trust in Him, we thwart the guiles of the evil one. And in those moments when we don't understand what we see and experience heartbreak over what we do, God's marvelous grace turns into a healing balm that enables us to love on others when that is the last thing we want to do.

Today, the Lord is not leading me to end my marriage. Which to many, including myself, is illogical. Waves of fear and doubt *dare* me to trust God for an amazing miracle and risk looking foolish . . . again. Though fluctuating emotions still take their toll, the turbulent extremes have disappeared. I now wake up each day believing the unbelievable—*because it's only unbelievable if I don't believe it.*

Keeping spiritually fed increases my confidence in the Lord, especially when it counters what I feel. Resources, such as *Fighting for Your Marriage While Separated* by Linda W. Rooks, motivate me to contend for my marriage while preventing the root of bitterness from grabbing hold of my spirit. And by working through the online course *Save My Marriage,*[165] I learn proven relationship-building tools and gain support to heal my wounded heart. Although this may sound paradoxical, when I take what I learn and pour it into others, that simple act of love fills my own heart and helps me stay focused and faithful.

We can learn much from those who have endured a similar path and emerged victorious. While saddened by the comparable stories of people like Lysa TerKeurst, Jill Savage, Jason Martinkus, Sheri Keffer, Joe Beam, and Leslie Vernick, their blogs, webinars, books, podcasts, and online programs encourage me to remain open to reconciliation and not hardened by resentment. I can now truly say, as did the apostle Paul, that I have learned to be content in any circumstance.[166]

I will always long for restoration, for a divine rebirth. For the point in the movie when the man walking away stops, turns around, and returns to what he needed and wanted all along. But no one epiphany altered our trajectory. No therapist. No weekend intensive. No prayer meeting. And regardless of how hard I try or how much I love Clark, it appears to most our marriage has failed.

Recently a friend told me, "Anything worth doing is worth doing poorly." At first the comment sounded crazy. *Why would you want to do anything poorly?* Then I recalled learning to sing—I couldn't read music, had difficulty finding the right pitch, and regularly forgot the words. My early days on the basketball court typified the same—I had no left hand, couldn't make a free throw, possessed no grasp of the game, and thought if I could see the rim I should shoot the ball.

Anything worth doing is worth doing poorly, and on occasion, for years.

Maybe you are struggling with your own poor performance, weary that the end is nowhere in sight. Be assured that as you *dare* to break through the fear and step out in faith to think, speak, and act on your belief in the unbelievable, month after month and year after year, the Lord will sustain you with courageous power just when you want to bail, and will pour into your soul a deeper revelation of Himself that cannot be shaken. I am living proof.

I choose to believe marriage is worth fighting for, faith is worth standing in, and Jesus is worth pursuing even when done poorly.

Faith to What End?

Amid the anxiousness of an uncertain future, the Text repeatedly calms my fears and guides me to the next right step. Still some passages confuse, exasperate, and even anger me. (I probably shouldn't be angry at the Bible.) Hebrews 11, often referred to as the Hall of Faith, is one of those chapters. It tells of the incredible faith of Abel, Enoch, Noah, Abraham, Isaac, Jacob, Sarah, Joseph, Moses, and Rahab. The author writes:

What more shall I say? For time would fail me to tell of Gideon, Barak, Samson, Jephthah, of David and Samuel and the prophets—who through faith conquered kingdoms, enforced justice, obtained promises, stopped the mouths of lions, quenched the power of fire, escaped the edge of the sword, were made strong out of weakness, became mighty in war, put foreign armies to flight. [Even w]omen received back their dead by resurrection.[167]

Stunning! My spirit is lit up just by typing the words. I long to live a life worthy of being on that list. Then I keep reading.

Some were tortured, refusing to accept release, so that they might rise again to a better life. Others suffered mocking and flogging, and even chains and imprisonment. They were stoned, they were sawn in two, they were killed with the sword. They went about in skins of sheep and goats, destitute, afflicted, mistreated—of whom the world was not worthy—wandering about in deserts and mountains, and in dens and caves of the earth.

And all these, though commended through their faith, did not receive what was promised, since God had provided something better for us, that apart from us they should not be made perfect.[168]

Right.

What do you do with that? What do you mean they did not receive what was promised? I would love for the first half of Hebrews 11 to be my reality but not the second half! I want to see the goodness of the Lord in the land of the living. I desire a thriving marriage, children who passionately follow Jesus, and an unwavering faith in God. I want to exhibit enough audacity, wisdom, and faith to merit a mention in the Bible and have even told the Lord as much.

Then one day I heard Him say, *Do you really desire a life worth reference in the Text? How about one like that of Hosea? Or Job?*

Seriously? I was thinking more like Ruth, who through obedience ended up with a husband who adored her, or Esther, who risked her life for others and became queen, or Mary, who said yes to God and raised His perfect Son!

Aarrgghh!

"Hebrews 11 is not about the greatness of humanity. It's about the goodness and grace of God to use broken and faulty people to accomplish His purposes. Sometimes in collaboration with their efforts, and sometimes despite their efforts."[169] God, out of His kindness and favor frequently chooses to partner with flawed people like you and me (and every other person in the Text) despite our failings or present situation. And even though we fall into the category of woefully inadequate, the Lord masterfully refashions anyone willing to follow Him.

The individuals described in the second half of Hebrews 11 exemplified a faith just as amazing as those in the first group—maybe even more so—and they suffered incognito. They didn't even garner a name drop. What if God calls us to walk in faith and not receive what was promised in our lifetime? To stand in faith and never see the vision fulfilled? To at no time be recognized or applauded? To keep pushing the rock when it's not going to move?

What if *daring* in faith costs you? What if it costs your career to stand up for your beliefs, a better car to tithe, a relationship to remain pure, your life to sacrifice for another? Will you *dare* pray and persevere in faith for what you may not see an answer to?

Faith will never make sense.

Abel, Adam's righteous second son, offered an acceptable sacrifice to the Lord yet was killed by his jealous brother for doing what the Lord desired, for doing what was right.[170] Just because we do the right thing doesn't mean the right thing will happen to us. I know the Lord's eternal promises will all come to pass, but until then am I willing to follow Him, loving others when I don't feel like it, if it means my name will be added to the second list? Even if it means the right thing may not happen to me?

I want to be willing . . .

We all realize it's not a matter of *if* we experience adversity but *when*. And the validity of God's call or purpose for us cannot be judged by whether we struggle through illness, deal with the repercussion of addiction, or try to recover from the devastation of divorce. Trials, hardship, and difficulty are all part of a divine process of transformation. Everyone in God's Hall of Faith endured physical and emotional affliction, some to the point of tortuous death. And they were right where God wanted them to be, becoming exactly whom He designed them to be.

Still, when unnerved by a sudden reality that lands us in an unfamiliar place, it's natural to ask God, *Why*? Why the pain? Why the delay? Why the heartache?

Truthfully, we may never know. But as we come to the end of this book, we are left to determine how we will walk out a faith that *dares*. How will we respond to our disappointment and pain? I like how the apostle Paul, imprisoned for sharing the gospel and sent on a cargo ship bound for trial in Rome, responded to finding himself shipwrecked on the isle of Malta.[171]

Stranded in a place he never planned to visit by fierce storms no one saw coming, Paul was bit by a viper as he helped to place wood on a fire. The Text says the poisonous snake fastened itself to his hand. It wasn't letting go. The natives quickly determined that although Paul escaped from the wreckage at sea, he must be a murderer and the gods would not allow him to live.

People (like most who watch from a distance) come to their own conclusions as to why we go through what we go through. We must have messed up or be guilty of some glaring sin. It's an innate reaction. I've done it too. Even more common is our own assumption that if we serve God well and follow Him, He should protect us from the shipwreck, the snake bite, the harmful words.

But Paul didn't argue with the well-meaning (though disillusioned) people, post complaints on social media, or try to defend himself. He just shook the snake off his hand and into the fire. When life hung in the balance and people barraged him with negativity, he shook off the snake. I need to get better at that. I need to stop taking a vote over what to do following a trial, when the unexpected bites, or when words are destructive. I just need to shake it off.

The Text says the people on the island watched Paul for a long time after the viper struck. Rather than offer assistance, they remained content to observe the drama. (Sound familiar?) When they noticed he didn't fall down dead, they changed their minds. He must be a god! Following the precipitous reversal from murderer to deity, Paul ended up called to the home of the chief man of the island and for three days, Paul shared Jesus. He prayed and laid hands on the sick and they were healed. The same hand that days earlier had been bit by a snake was now being used by God to cure disease.

God had told Paul he was going to Rome, and Paul rested on that truth. He believed the Lord even when his circumstances appeared contradictory. I am comforted to know that by sharing Jesus amid the life-altering storms of broken dreams, unforeseen pain, and misdirected comments, courage and restoration extends to the wounded.

Maybe you have found yourself stuck where it's rainy, cold, and unfamiliar, where despite good intentions you feel attacked and misunderstood. Be assured that the Lord will use every piece of our disappointing journey and the sting of significant loss to bring hope and healing to those who are hurting. Though we may not understand, we can choose to walk out a faith that *dares* by using our own painful trial to draw others to Jesus. And while we wait until God opens the next door (or puts us on the next ship), we can continue to praise Him in the hallway. Like the psalmist David, let's "Be strong and courageous, all you who put your hope in the Lord!" [172]

Plant the Tree Anyway

Shortly after settling a dispute with Abimelech at Beersheba, Abraham planted a tamarisk tree. [173] In the Negev desert a tamarisk tree must send its taproot nearly one-hundred-feet deep to find a water source before much growth is visible on the surface. Decades will pass before anyone sits under its shade.

Abraham wasn't planting the tree for himself; he was planting it for his descendants. He was trusting the story. As one writer stated, "He was believing God's promise and staking a claim." [174] By planting the tamarisk tree, Abraham made a statement of faith that the generations to come would indeed live in this land. And every moment we step forward in *daring* and enduring faith—allowing our roots to grow deeper in Jesus—we are making one too.

Trees (like us) benefit from more than just deep roots. Giant sequoias in the California Redwood Forest last for millennia because their roots, which lie only six-to-twelve inches from the surface, extend nearly 150 feet from the base of each tree. The roots intertwine with those of other trees in the grove, enabling the sequoias to survive harsh weather. [175]

I am humbled by deep-rooted relationships that bolster me to stand in faith and finish well; grateful the Lord prepared Spirit-led women to intertwine their faith with mine, just as others walked away. My community, a precious grove, want God's best for Clark and for me. They pray for our relationship to work, ask the hard questions, and lovingly provide stability and protection on days when I find it difficult to endure.

Maybe your current circumstance tempts you to admit defeat and bail. Ask the Holy Spirit to enable you to plant a tree even if its shade will never fall on you; to send your roots deep no matter how long it takes; to weave your roots together with those of other believers. This might look like praying for those who have hurt you, talking through the pain of your story, or joining a support group. And after you step out in faith, trust the Lord to help you stand firm in the storm.

Throughout the Text the Lord repeatedly empowered women—like Hannah, Abigail, Jael, and the Samaritan at the well—to boldly live out their faith. Proverbs 31:10 says, "Who can find a virtuous woman?"[176] In Hebrew, the word for virtuous is *hayil*. It is synonymous to words like *valiant, might, strong, power*. Strong's Concordance defines it with the phrase, *probably a force*.[177] I love that. Regardless of the trial, we can be a virtuous force on the earth that *dares* to wage war against the temptation to complain, criticize, sulk, or wither away.

Make up your mind to step out in His power and stay the course when others won't. After all, the Bible, while a story meant for us, is not about us. It is God's awesome story; it is all about Him. *Dare* to let your story not be about you. *Dare* to go deep even if it means you may not see the result of what you are standing for in your generation. Plant the tree, trusting the Lord as you—

Reach out in your pain.
Forgive when it's difficult.

Love when it feels impossible.

Give out of lack.

Believe for supernatural healing.

Mine the Text.

Reflect Jesus to friends and colleagues.

Pursue a Presence-directed marriage.

Raise children to follow Jesus.

Make an eternal difference in this world.

A Divine Vision

As much as we may choose to embrace God-given dreams and visions, we cannot have faith in faith, or faith in our works, or faith in what we envision. True and *daring* faith loves God and leans fully on Him when we don't know the next step, when dreams are shattered, and the crutch of our efforts falls away. For it is not the greatness of my faith or yours that will change our lives, it is the greatness of the Lord abiding in us. And as we remain faithful, our vision will transform into His.

Decades removed from challenges I once deemed unbearable—suffering through breakups, losing a job, waiting for Mitch, and now facing a crumbling relationship—I have come to realize God's divine vision for my life is way different than I imagined. Yes, the Spirit taught me to radically forgive, to expect healing, to traverse a wilderness, to hold fast to my marriage, all while believing for a tangible vision. But the truth is, the vision I hold today of a healed marriage is not guaranteed. And should that end up my reality, did I miss God's plan for me?

Emphatically, no!

Through this surprising and ofttimes arduous journey of standing in faith, the Lord unexpectedly transformed my heart while leading me into a depth of intimacy with Him I never knew possible. I thought the fulfillment of my vision was the end goal, but His divine vision was always to draw me closer to Him. Relationship is what He wanted all along. It's what He enjoyed in the garden with Adam and Eve, with His friend Abraham, when He talked to Moses face-to-face, as He dwelt among His people in the tabernacle, and what was embodied by Jesus, who spent more than thirty years pouring His life into relationships. It's what the Lord fervently pursued with Mary at the tomb, with the men on the road to Emmaus, and with the disciples back in Galilee.

Why should I be surprised that knowing the Lord is really His ultimate vision for us all?

Choosing to pursue a growing and personal relationship with our adoring heavenly Father, opens the door for Him to gift each of us with the ability to press on when it looks impossible. And in our *daring* expression of faith, we will discover He is who He says He is, and He will do what He says He will do.

My hope rests in knowing Jesus is still on the throne and He will relentlessly love us through all we encounter. The presence of the Lord will not disappoint, regardless of which half of Hebrews 11 my name falls. There are days I yearn to see Jesus coming in the clouds, and other days I pray His mercy and grace lasts for generations. Either way, we are in the race of our lives, and we have the sweet honor of running the anchor leg. *Dare* to stay the course through the final lap; *dare* to walk in what you know is real; *dare* to live as though every word of the Text is true, ignoring the potential darkness tomorrow may bring. You don't have to have hope to *dare* in faith. *Daring* in faith will produce hope.

I would love to conclude this book with "And they lived happily ever after." But what do you expect from a title, *When Faith Dares*? How do I *dare* write about potential risk and failure if neither are real? How do we discover the power of courage to stay the course when we'd rather bail, without a valid reason to bail? I don't know whether my marriage will survive. Nevertheless, I choose to trust the Lord with my heart, my life, my husband, and my family. And when the onslaught of negativity feels insurmountable and I don't see His hand moving, there's Jesus. I *dare* believe that He is doing a new thing; that He will make a way in the wilderness and rivers in the desert.[178] That "to all who mourn in Israel, he will give a crown of beauty for ashes, a joyous blessing instead of mourning, festive praise instead of despair. In their righteousness, they will be like great oaks that the Lord has planted for his own glory."[179]

Yes, the Lord is planting trees too.

From the first day I experienced a vision of God high up in my backyard tree fort, I assumed fulfillment meant my dreams would come true. But no amount of success in our short time here on earth (however we want to measure that) will ever compare with a greater revelation and awareness of the Lord's presence in our lives. It all takes a back seat to knowing the love of Jesus, talking with Him, entrusting Him with our very lives. For His abiding presence fills us with a hope that will *never* disappoint, no matter what happens.

More to this narrative will yet unfold as Clark walks a road unlike any I have ever known. And though the outcome is uncertain, God is not. For if we refuse to live as though the Lord can change people and convert a terrible situation into something incredible, then we don't believe the gospel. To date, the greatest thing the Spirit of God ever empowered me to do is to love Clark; to reflect the passion of Jesus by remaining committed to that relationship. I know the Lord will refashion every heart that is willing, because I have seen Him do it to mine.

The story I've told in this book and now the story displayed through the living of our lives requires a creative imagination, a divine vision, a listening spirit, and a belief in the impossible. It will demand we grant radical forgiveness, wait well in the valley, and long to be in

His house. And whether our path forward is foreseen or unexpected, the Lord will purify our hearts as we relinquish our agenda and chase after Him. Then one day—even when our heart is breaking—we will find our faith has radiantly grown to *dare* believe the unbelievable.

And we will come to know Jesus.

I pray you experience the eternal life described in John 17:3: "to know (to perceive, recognize, become acquainted with, and understand) You, the only true and real God, and [likewise] to know Him, Jesus [as the] Christ (the Anointed One, the Messiah), Whom You have sent."[180] And should the unfolding of my life allow me to express, "The path ahead is long and hard, and Jesus is our hope!" in a way that inspires you to chase after Him with all your heart, soul, mind, and strength . . . I would do it all over again.

As you embody a faith that *dares,* your story line will prove unpredictable. But through it all, the Spirit of the Lord who resides in your heart will embolden you to stand in faith for the improbable. You now know truth, and what will satisfy others will not satisfy you. Regardless of the whirlwind that threatens to blow you away, God will keep you in perfect peace when you abandon yourself to His divine vision and place your trust in Him.[181]

Dare to hold a miraculous image of restoration. And even if it doesn't turn out exactly how you envision, you can still say with confidence, **I. Trust. In. You. God.**

Because this is *when faith dares.*

Appendix

Prayer of Commitment

When we embrace the truth of the Good News of the gospel—the life, death, burial, and resurrection of Jesus Christ for the forgiveness of our sins—a process of transformation begins. By sincerely expressing your heart to the Lord God through the sample prayer below, you will embark on your own personal relationship with Him, and you will never be the same.

Dear heavenly Father,

For too long my sin has kept me separated from You. I believe You sent Your Son, Jesus, to bear the penalty of my disobedience by dying on the cross. I believe He rose from the dead for the forgiveness of my sin and is alive right now hearing my prayer. Today I humbly call out to You, tired of doing things my own way, and invite Jesus to be my Lord and Savior. Fill the God-shaped hole in my life with Your Holy Spirit and empower me to follow You well. I pray You will create in me a clean heart that desires to bring You glory. Give me the grace to draw close to You and to experience Your kingdom here on earth as it is in heaven. Thank You for loving me and for adopting me into Your family. I am your child because of Jesus. Amen.

If you have made the life-altering decision to follow Jesus, whether for the first time or you're now returning home, we would love to encourage you on your faith journey. Please contact us at *terrimcfarland.org*.

Reference List

1. Matthew 4:19
2. Genesis 11:6, KJV.
3. 1 Corinthians 2:9
4. John 20:29
5. See Luke 1:37; John 14:14; John 14:12; John 14:2.
6. KJV.
7. Oswald Chambers, "Vision and Reality," *My Utmost for His Highest*, July 6, https://utmost.org/classic/vision-and-reality-classic/. Reprinted with permission.
8. John 14:12
9. Proverbs 29:18, AMP.
10. Philippians 4:19
11. Matthew 19:19
12. Titus 1:2; Hebrews 13:8
13. 1 Samuel 28; Jonah 1; Acts 5
14. NIV.
15. Genesis 22; Joshua 10; 1 Samuel 17
16. Steven Furtick, *Sun Stand Still: What Happens When You Dare to Ask God for the Impossible* (Colorado Springs, CO: Multnomah, 2010), 25.
17. Randy Alcorn, "Florence Chadwick and the Fog," Eternal Perspective Ministries, January 21, 2010, www.epm.org/resources/2010/jan/21/florence-chadwick-and-fog.

18. Matthew 14

19. Psalm 139:16

20. Matthew 19:26

21. Psalm 37:4

22. Jim Abbott, one-armed MLB pitcher for the Angels, Yankees, White Sox, and Brewers from 1989-1999. Check out my one-handed YouTube video, Terri McFarland Softball, https://www.youtube.com/watch?v=05xEiNVW3IU.

23. You can read more about that experience in their book, *Total Freedom: Experiencing supernatural victory through Jesus Christ* by Armour and Siola McFarland (Lulu.com, 2011).

24. John 5:30

25. Deuteronomy 34:10

26. Hebrews 13:8

27. Marcus Warner, *Understanding the Wounded Heart* (Carmel, IN: Deeper Walk International, 2013), 56.

28. Isaiah 54:17

29. Psalm 46:10

30. 1 Thessalonians 5:17

31. Rachel Sugar, Richard Feloni, and Ashley Lutz, "Twenty-nine Famous People Who Failed Before They Succeeded," Businessinsider.com, July 9, 2015, https://www.businessinsider.com/successful-people-who-failed-at-first-2015-7.

32. John 11:39

33. 1 Samuel 17:28

34. Romans 4:18

35. Romans 8:11

36. See Matthew 5:44.

37. Psalm 37:3

38. See Nehemiah 8:10.

39. *The Interpreter*, Universal Pictures, 2005.

40. Tim Mackie, "27. Forgiveness (Matthew)," at 20:00 mark, https://www.youtube.com/watch?v=c89o7NaR7zI.

41. James 2:13

42. Proverbs 28:9, AMP.

43. Strongs G863, *Blue Letter Bible*, accessed September 9, 2020, https://www.blueletterbible.org/lang/lexicon/lexicon.cfm?Strongs=G863&t=ESV.

44. You can find wonderful resources on navigating challenging relationships at leslievernick.com, drcloud.com, or drtownsend.com.

45. Galatians 5:1

46. Oswald Chambers, *My Utmost for His Highest*, July 6 entry, Vision and Reality; https://utmost.org/classic/vision-and-reality-classic/.

47. Mark 4:35

48. Mark 4:40

49. Psalm 23:4

50. Genesis 11

51. Genesis 12:1

52. James 1:2

53. Exodus 25:8

54. See Genesis 32.

55. Professor Jonathan Lipnick, "The Authentic Hebrew Meaning of the Word *Israel*," Israel Institute of Biblical Studies, https://www.youtube.com/watch?v=GLeifwpjf2E.

56. Matt Fitzgerald, *How Bad Do You Want It?: Mastering the Psychology of Mind over Muscle* (Boulder, CO: Velopress, 2015), 204–5.

57. Exodus 17:13

58. Strongs H530, emuwnah, Blue Letter Bible, https://www.blueletterbible.org/lang/lexicon/lexicon.cfm?Strongs=H530&t=ESV.

59. See Proverbs 18:24.

60. See 1 Kings 18–19.

61. underthefigtree.org

62. Psalm 24:9

63. Mark 4:41

64. See Joshua 10.

65. See Hebrews 13:5; Lamentations 3:22-23.

66. Isaiah 49:23, NIV.

67. Luke Ward, *How Much Time People Spend Doing Stuff in Their Lifetime*, thefactsite.com, Thefactsite.com, accessed October 5, 2020, https://www.thefactsite.com/how-much-time-people-spend-doing-stuff.

68. Athletes in Action is the athletic division of Cru.

69. Isaiah 55:8

70. See Genesis 15.

71. Joshua 1:2, 5

72. See Joshua 3.

73. Joshua 1:9

74. Bodie Hodge, Answers in Genesis, "How Long Did It Take for Noah to Build the Ark?," June 10, 2010, https://answersingenesis.org/bible-timeline/how-long-did-it-take-for-noah-to-build-the-ark/.

75. See Luke 1.

76. Isaiah 40:31

77. Matthew 6:21

78. Mark 4:26-27

79. Ann Kiemel Anderson, *Ordinary Days*, accessed October 10, 2020, http://www.appleseeds.org/Ordinary_Days.htm.

80. Galatians 5:22

81. Galatians 6:9

82. Genesis 15:5

83. See Genesis 17.

84. See Genesis 37.

85. See Exodus 2.

86. See Luke 15.

87. Luke 15:17-19, my paraphrase.

88. Luke 15:31

89. See Exodus 24.

90. Exodus 24:12

91. Ibid.

92. Strongs 1961, Biblehub.com, accessed November 21, 2020, https://biblehub.com/interlinear/exodus/24-12.htm.

93. Larry Christenson, *The Renewed Mind: Becoming the Person God Wants You to Be* (Bloomington, MN: Bethany House Publishers, 1974, 2001), 11.

94. Habakkuk 2:2

95. See Exodus 17.

96. Kathy Troccoli, "A Different Road," Reunion Records, *Corner of Eden* album, 1998.

97. Matthew 8:5-13; 8:24-27; 9:18-19, 23-26; 9:27-34; Mark 5:1-20; 5:25-34; Luke 7:12-16.

98. Mark 6:37

99. See John 11.

100. Mark 9:24

101. Russell Kelso Carter, "Standing on the Promises," copyright 1886, public domain.

102. George DeJong, *In A Word: Lessons from the Language of the Wilderness* (Holland, MI: Under the Fig Tree Ministries, 2015), 13.

103. *Bible Encyclopedia*, ChristianAnswers.net, Desert, accessed December 7, 2020, https://christiananswers.net/dictionary/desert.html.

104. Ibid.

105. Strong's H4057, *midbar*, Blue Letter Bible, accessed December 7, 2020, https://www.blueletterbible.org/lang/lexicon/lexicon.cfm?Strongs=H4057&t=ESV.

106. Deuteronomy 8:2

107. Philippians 4:7

108. See 1 Samuel 15; 2 Samuel 11; John 18.

109. See Genesis 27, 38.

110. See Exodus 2; Judges 13-16; Matthew 26; Luke 18.

111. H. Norman Wright, *When the Past Won't Let You Go: Finding the Healing that Helps You Move On* (Eugene, OR: Harvest House Publishers, 2016), 64.

112. See Ruth 1–4; Esther 5; Luke 10.

113. See Genesis 46:2; Jonah 4.

114. See Joel 2:25.

115. Wright, *When the Past Won't Let You Go*, 43–44.

116. 2 Corinthians 10:5

117. Dr. Caroline Leaf, *Switch On Your Brain: The Key to Peak Happiness, Thinking, and Health* (Grand Rapids, MI: Baker Books, 2013), 33.

118. Romans 12:2

119. Colossians 3:2

120. Proverbs 23:7, NKJV.

121. Romans 4:17, AMPC.

122. Psalm 42:5, NIV.

123. Mo Costandi, "Reflecting on Mirror Neurons," *The Guardian*, August 23, 2013, https://www.theguardian.com/science/neurophilosophy/2013/aug/23/mirror-neurons.

124. Matthew 6:22

125. See Genesis 30.

126. Proverbs 3:5-6

127. See Deuteronomy 24:5.

128. See Psalm 139.

129. See Mark 1:35.

130. See Genesis 16:3; Joshua 9; 1 Samuel 23:14; 1 Samuel 28; 1 Kings 11:3.

131. See Judges 21:25.

132. Brad Gray, *Make Your Mark: Getting Right What Samson Got Wrong* (New York: Faith Words, 2014), 148.

133. See Daniel 6; Acts 7, 14.

134. See 1 Samuel 17.

135. See Zechariah 4:10.

136. Wayne Stiles, *Waiting on God: What to Do When God Does Nothing* (Grand Rapids, MI: Baker, 2015), 110.

137. See Hebrews 11:6.

138. Habakkuk 2:3

139. See Romans 11:29.

140. 1 Timothy 2:3-4

141. Psalm 139:23-24, NIV.

142. Philippians 1:29

143. Strong's G5483, *Blue Letter Bible*, accessed February 5, 2021, https://www.blueletterbible.org/lang/lexicon/lexicon.cfm?Strongs=G5483&t=ESV.

144. See 1 Corinthians 10:13.

145. See 2 Corinthians 12:9.

146. See Philippians 4:19.

147. See Luke 10:19.

148. See Ephesians 1:18-19.

149. Romans 8:37, NKJV.

150. See Psalm 51:10.

151. Luke 18:27

152. See Exodus 17.

153. See Jeremiah 29:13.

154. tlmministries.com

155. See Luke 5.

156. See Matthew 14.

157. See Genesis 12.

158. See Acts 13.

159. See Luke 15.

160. Leslie Vernick, *The Emotionally Destructive Marriage: How to Find Your Voice and Reclaim Your Hope* (Colorado Springs, CO: WaterBrook Press, 2013), 1.

161. Matthew 9:2; Matthew 9:22; Mark 6:50.

162. See Romans 8:28.

163. Ezekiel 37:3

164. See 1 Kings 18:44.

165. Offered at MarriageHelper.com

166. See Philippians 4:11.

167. Hebrews 11:32-35

168. Hebrews 11:35-40

169. Brad Gray, *Make Your Mark: Getting Right What Samson Got Wrong* (New York: Faith Words, 2014), 170.

170. See Genesis 4; Hebrews 11:4.

171. See Acts 28.

172. Psalm 31:24

173. See Genesis 21:22-34.

174. Marty Solomon, "Trees of the Desert: Ar'ar & Tamarisk," *Covered in His Dust* blog, November 13, 2013, http://makingtal-midim.blogspot.com/2013/11/trees-of-desert-arar-tamarisk.html.

175. Angela Cahill, *Nature's Masterpiece: Giant Sequoia*, Pacific Horticulture Society, October 2000, https://www.pacifichorticul-ture.org/articles/natures-masterpiece-giant-sequoia/.

176. KJV.

177. Strong's H2428, *Blue Letter Bible*, accessed May 21, 2021, https://www.blueletterbible.org/lang/lexicon/lexicon.cfm?Strongs=H2428&t=ESV.

178. See Isaiah 43:19.

179. Isaiah 61:3, NLT.

180. AMPC.

181. See Isaiah 26:3.

Acknowledgments

Words fail to adequately describe my gratitude to You, my heavenly Father, for opening doors and leading me through. When I don't understand and don't see Your plan, You lovingly and faithfully guide me right where You want me to go. I am forever changed by my journey of faith with You—the One whose hands so tenderly hold my heart.

To George DeJong, your hunger to dive deep into the Text overflows to my spirit and repeatedly changes the way I view the heart of our God. Thank you for being faithful to your call in such a way that it blesses mine.

To the board members of TLM Ministries: Michael, Gina, Robin, Beth Ann, and Ken, thank you for encouraging me to tell my story and for covering me in prayer through it all.

To those who stood the test of time, faithfully supporting me through the laughter, heartache, and tears, thank you! Lauri, Tonya, Lyn, Ron, Angie, Michael, Cindy, Monica, Kayti, Jorgi, LaVerna, Michele, Amps, Mo, Heidi, Deb, Marguerite, Scott, Pastor James, Malachi, Darby, Tracy, and all the women in my precious small group, you continue to steady my arms in the battle. Hold on my dear friends because we win!

To Ginger Kolbaba, you believed in me when I wasn't sure this book would ever make literary sense. I am forever grateful for your editorial expertise, kind heart, and incredible wisdom in a process so foreign to me. You were a gift! My heart is broken that you never saw this project come to fruition, yet your fingerprints lie on every page.

To Kathy Bruins, you stepped in at just the right time to add the finishing touches to this book. Thank you for sharing your enormous talents and passion with me.

To Heidi Harrington, your artistic creativity remains unmatched and your faith inspiring. I am blessed to be a recipient of both.

To Clark, Ryan, Ben, Grace, and the rest of my family—thank you for allowing the Lord to place me in your lives. I will never be the same.

And to the thousands of students, athletes, and amazing women I have had the privilege of pouring into over the years, thank you for trusting me with your own *daring* story of faith. My heart is full.

About the Author

Terri McFarland serves as a Bible teacher, Christian recording artist, worship leader, and conference speaker, traveling around the world to share the hope found in Jesus. She regularly partners with Under the Fig Tree Ministries to facilitate tours to the Middle East and teams up with the Fellowship of Christian Athletes in a variety of capacities. As a former collegiate and international athlete and coach, Terri delights in the opportunity to influence those willing to chase after Jesus with the passion of an athlete pursuing their sport. Through her own story of heartbreaking loss and disappointment, Terri *dares* to hold on to Jesus Christ, believing in every situation, the beauty of His faithfulness will be revealed.

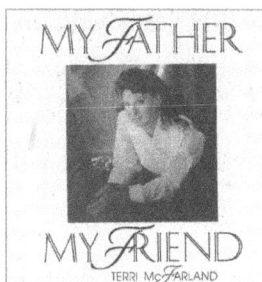

www.ingramcontent.com/pod-product-compliance
Lightning Source LLC
Chambersburg PA
CBHW071215090426
42736CB00014B/2824